Praise for *True Tales from the Campaign Trail*

This collection of stories from the campaign trail is a fun read, with some important implicit messages for students of politics woven throughout. The first-hand accounts from different perspectives—operatives, candidates, reporters, and others—tell about the rich variation in US campaign politics, with accounts from urban and rural America, all regions, and contests ranging from the most obscure to the presidency. These accounts span decades, but some things are timeless: failures are as instructive as successes, and campaigns revolve around people, sometimes ones who would appear to have no overt connection to the political world. There's a particularly good takeaway for this current era with its celebration of data, analytics and the science of campaigns: Politics is every bit *art* as it is *science*. And for scholars and students, these accounts offer real-word grist for their understanding of campaign politics.

—Barbara Trish, Professor of Political Science, Grinnell College

True Tales from the Campaign Trail
Stories Only Political Consultants Can Tell

Volume 3

Written and compiled by Jerry Austin

University of Akron Press
Akron, Ohio

All inquiries and permission requests should be addressed to the Publisher, The University of Akron Press, Akron, Ohio 44325-1703.

ISBN: 978-1-62922-263-9 (paper)
ISBN: 978-1-62922-264-6 (ePDF)
ISBN: 978-1-62922-265-3 (ePub)

A catalog record for this title is available from the Library of Congress.

∞ The paper used in this publication meets the minimum requirements of ANSI/NISO z39.48–1992 (Permanence of Paper).

Cover design and illustration: Doug Granger

True Tales from the Campaign Trail was designed and typeset in Adobe Caslon with Futura display by Amy Freels. *True Tales from the Campaign Trail* was printed on sixty-pound white and bound by Bookmasters of Ashland, Ohio.

Contents

III. Political People

Introduction

The journey of *True Tales from the Campaign Trail* began in 1999.

I had an idea: What if I asked political consultants of my generation to write a few of their best stories to be included in a book of political stories entitled, *You Can't Make This Up*? The stories would be published, and the proceeds would be used to fund a fellowship for a college student to be embedded in a campaign and learn politics as a practicum.

Only one consultant, David Heller, replied with a few of his stories (some of which are included in this book). I abandoned the project but wrote my stories thinking my kids and grandkids may be interested after I'm gone.

Jump ahead fifteen years. I'm an adjunct professor at The Bliss Institute of Applied Politics at The University of Akron. I asked the director, Dr. John Green, if the institute would fund my pursuit of these political stories via one-on-one interviews with longtime political consultants and political journalists. He said yes.

My modus operandi was to interview the consultants and journalists while recording their stories. I interviewed Democrats and Republicans; many I knew, and others I did not. The sessions lasted from two to four hours, which included turning off the recorder and telling my own stories to the interviewee.

The tapes were to be transcribed by Bliss students, edited by Dr. Green, and published by The University of Akron Press.

Unfortunately, the sportscaster Al Michael's autobiography was using the original title *You Can't Make This Up*. And thus, *True Tales from the Campaign Trail* was published, followed by Volume 2, and now Volume 3.[*]

I would like to thank my fellow consultants who shared their stories, Doug Granger for designing the covers for all three volumes, and the staffs of the Bliss Institute and University of Akron Press for their assistance.

I invite you, the readers, to enjoy these stories and write your own.

We all have stories to tell.

Gerald "Jerry" Austin
Tallmadge, Ohio
Spring 2022

---

[*] Jerry Austin, *True Tales from the Campaign Trail*, Vol. 1., Akron, Ohio, The University of Akron Press, 2017, and *True Tales from the Campaign Trail*, Vol. 2., Akron, Ohio, The University of Akron Press, 2021.

I. Buckeye Politics

Tale of the Tape

Jerry Austin

My first statewide consulting gig was in 1978. I was hired to manage and do the media for State Senator Anthony J. "Tony" Celebrezze, Jr., who was challenging longtime Republican incumbent Ted Brown for Ohio secretary of state (SOS).

Celebrezze was the son of Anthony J. Celebrezze, former Cleveland mayor and secretary of Health Education and Welfare during the Kennedy Administration.

Brown had been elected and reelected SOS since 1950. The Brown name was gold for Ohio Republicans for decades, with numerous candidates benefiting from having that last name. In 1958, Republicans lost every statewide office due to a business-sponsored right-to-work ballot issue—except Ted Brown. And in 1970, only Ted Brown—and Lieutenant Governor John Brown—survived a Democratic landslide.

Beating Ted Brown was a long shot.

In the past, candidates ran against Brown based upon his record as SOS. No one came close. I decided to authorize a poll to learn what the voters knew about the office of SOS. It was a very short poll that did not ask the "horse race" question between the Celebrezze and Brown campaigns. Instead, the major question was "Which of the following is the main responsibility of the SOS?" The choices: "Represents Ohio at the United Nations;" "Ohio's chief elections officer;" or "Head of the

Secretaries Association of Ohio." Three-quarters of the respondents chose "Represents Ohio at the United Nations."

I knew my only issue was that Brown had served for twenty years and was seventy-two years old. Using age as an issue is a very chancy strategy. How do you not offend seniors who are the largest group of voters? Because Celebrezze did not have a primary for the Democratic nomination for SOS, I had several months to develop a communication plan using age as the main message.

Finally, due to pure luck, I had a plan.

While seated at the bar eating dinner at a local Columbus bistro, a news story came on the TV about the upcoming heavyweight championship boxing contest between Muhammed Ali and Leon Spinks. During the story, a visual was put on the screen titled "The Tale of the Tape."

A picture of each candidate was on the screen side by side. Underneath was a comparison of their height, weight, biceps, and records.

I had my strategy: I would compare Brown and Celebrezze using age and other categories, such as education and experience.

I sent an intern to Brown's office to ask for a photo of the SOS. The receptionist gladly handed over an 8 x 12 black and white photo. Good luck: black and white instead of color. To compare Brown's still black and white photo, I would use moving color footage of Celebrezze.

Next, I decided to use a different voiceover for each candidate: a strong male voice for Celebrezze and a weak female voice for Brown. (Hey, it was 1978.)

I booked an edit suite with the Media Group in Columbus. The ad was easy to produce.

Education? Still black and white of Brown on the screen; weak female voiceover: "Attended Wittenberg College."

Moving color footage of Celebrezze talking to a group of elderly women on the screen; strong male voiceover: "Graduate of U.S. Naval Academy."

Footage on screen then dissolved into a picture of Tony's father being sworn in as cabinet secretary by President Kennedy; to the left of JFK was Midshipman Tony Celebrezze in his dress Navy whites.

Experience? "Celebrezze, chosen one of Ohio's best legislators" and "Brown, the incumbent." The female voiceover said "incumbent" as if it was a disease.

Age? Celebrezze thirty-seven; Brown seventy-two.

"Wait a minute," I said to my editor. "Can you make thirty-seven move to become seventy-three?"

He responded, "Yes, but he's only seventy-two."

I replied, "Do it. Brown will call a press conference and state he's only seventy-two."

I decided to preview my ad with the media. No one had done that in Ohio before. Reporters saw the spot and ran a story or news clip featuring the ad. Not one of the reporters knew Brown was seventy-two.

The spot aired, and Brown did call a press conference as anticipated. He said that his wife insisted he set the record straight—he was only seventy-two years old. His statement reinforced the message of the ad.

I also produced a radio ad featuring the voice of President Harry Truman. The voiceover declared, "In 1950, twenty-eight years ago, Harry Truman was president, and Ted Brown was elected secretary of state. Twenty-eight years ago."

Celebrezze won the general election by just over eight thousand votes. His victory is considered one of the greatest upsets in Ohio political history.

To my knowledge, the "Tale of the Tape" was the first comparison ad ever made, and certainly the first one in Ohio.

Credit Where Credit Was Due

Jerry Austin

A few years ago, I was in Buffalo having lunch with the late Joe Slade White, a great political consultant.

We talked about our first TV ads. I told him he was partly responsible for my first ad in 1978.

I was managing my first statewide race in Ohio of the secretary of state. My candidate, State Senator Tony Celebrezze, was running against a twenty-eight-year-old incumbent named Ted Brown.

I told Tony we had enough money for one TV spot. He said to find someone to do the spot.

I met with a few consultants in Washington, D.C., and eventually interviewed Joe in his New York City office/home. He showed me his reel of ads.

I asked how much it cost to produce one of his spots. He said $16,000. I replied that I meant just to produce, not including the buy. He said $16,000.

I returned to Ohio and told Tony I had found the person to do his ad.

He asked, "Who?"

I replied: "Me."

I told him I knew the state. I knew that the only issue in the race was age. And the spot would not cost $16,000.

He said, "You've never done an ad."

I said, "You've never run statewide. Roll the dice."

And he did.

My one ad was perhaps the first comparison spot ever made, and we won in a huge upset. Joe's response to my story was, "Glad I can take credit for your success!"

Followed by a huge laugh.

An Early Mistake Earns Free Media

Jerry Austin

One of my most embarrassing moments was during my first statewide race in Ohio. My candidate, Anthony Celebrezze, was unopposed in the Democratic primary to challenge an incumbent Republican secretary of state in the general election, Ted Brown. I had arranged an interview with a *National Public Radio* reporter in Columbus about our campaign.

At the time, I was going through a divorce and had just come to my last session of divorce counseling. As the interview began, out of nowhere I said, "I know it's tough to elect Tony Celebrezze because he looks like a mafia hit man." I went on with the interview and forgot that it would be on the radio three or four days later.

When the interview was played, absolute hell broke loose. A story was written in every newspaper in the state with the line, "Celebrezze's campaign manager calls him a hit man." A Republican County chairman in the Cleveland area got a tape of the interview and sent it to radio stations all over the state. The story ran for almost a week in July.

Despite my mistake, Celebrezze ended up winning the general election.

What I learned was that even though I made a bad mistake, it was only in the headlines for a week in July. By the time November came, nobody remembered what the headline was about, but they knew Tony Celebrezze's name because of all the free media.

Nail File
Jerry Austin

In 1978, Anthony Celebrezze was elected secretary of state in Ohio. It was a big upset. He beat the incumbent named Ted Brown, who had been in office for twenty-eight years.

On election night, Tony's small margin of victory led to an automatic recount. I went up to the secretary of state's office that evening to talk with Brown about what needed to be done—because he was going to be supervising the recount in his own race. Brown was drunk. Some verbal fisticuffs ensued, and I left. Tony eventually won the recount and the election.

During a transition period, the person who has won is usually invited to the office of the person they are succeeding. That never happened during this transition period. So, after Tony Celebrezze was sworn in as secretary of state, he went up to his new office for the first time. He'd never been there before.

Like most people, Tony walked into his new office, sat behind the desk, and pulled out different drawers. In the top drawer, he found twenty-eight years of nail clippings. Secretary Brown had clipped his nails, filed them in the top drawer, and left them as a token of his affection for his successor.

Tony found me within an hour and told me what he had found. I asked him why he was calling me—he should be calling housekeeping.

What Mattered to Ohio Voters

Terry Casey

James A. Rhodes was a fascinating character. He grew up poor in southern Ohio. He moved to Columbus and had an amazing rise in politics. He was elected to the school board and mayor of Columbus in the 1930s and 1940s. He went on to serve as Ohio State Auditor and governor of Ohio. He is the only Ohioan to serve in that office for four four-year terms—for a total of sixteen years.

So, Rhodes was a long-serving governor in a pivotal state, both politically and economically. In those days, most forms of transportation went through Ohio—rail, highways, shipping on Lake Erie and the Ohio River, even air travel before jets— linking the east with the rest of the country. Unlike most large states that were dominated by one or two large cities, Ohio was a collection of "city states." The worlds of Cleveland and Cincinnati both had heavy Catholic populations, with the same Pope and the same church, but were so different. Then there was Toledo, Dayton, Akron, and Youngstown, but there were also lots of smaller cities, like Mansfield, Portsmouth, Zanesville, and Lima. Each one was distinctive—and proud of it. People in Columbus thought they were the center of the universe because of the state capital, but, of course, the other cities said, "The heck with you, we're the 'capital of the tristate' or 'we're a world-class city.'" Ohio is still like that today but less pivotal because of the rise of the Sunbelt states.

Rhodes was a successful governor because he held executive offices before becoming governor. A lot of governors have been legislators, and they knew about making speeches and talking about issues, but not about hiring people, keeping an eye on people, and building a fire under people to get things done. Rhodes was a master of managing state government. He would have one meeting going, and he'd kind of drop in, and then he'd slide into another meeting. He'd kind of jockey back and forth. He would keep stoking the fire, getting people to do things. He knew inherently that you had to get bureaucrats—like businesspeople—focused on the bottom line. He could cut through the detail and the distraction. He once told a guy who was hemming and hawing about an issue, "Dammit, when I ask, what time is it? I want to know what time it is. I don't want to know how the watch works."

One of the things about Rhodes was that he understood politics: you're not as important as some people will tell you or you might like to assume. In June of 1982, Rhodes was just finishing his sixteenth year as governor. He was trying to tell a party leader and fundraiser what being governor meant when you are no longer the governor.

Rhodes said, "Next week, I'm going to be in Cincinnati, playing in this charity Pro-Am golf tournament. On Monday, I'll be in the first cart with Jack Nicklaus and Bob Hope. People will tell me I'm very important. But next year, I won't be governor, and then I'll be thirty-seven carts back, and most people will barely know my name, and nobody will pay attention to me."

In the 1980 Republican presidential primary, Rhodes hadn't announced who he was going to endorse. Then he scheduled a press conference with Ronald Reagan at the Governor's Mansion and endorsed Reagan. A reporter asked, "Well, Governor, why did you decide today on Sunday to endorse Ronald Reagan?" He gave an artful nonanswer, "Well, Saturday would have been too early, and Monday would have been too late." After that answer, how could a reporter ask a follow up question?

In the 1980 general election, Reagan was staying at the Neil House in Columbus to speak to a Teamsters convention. Reagan was getting questions about the islands off Taiwan—whether China controlled them or whether Taiwan controlled them. Rhodes had a famous session with Reagan where he whipped out his wallet, slammed it on the table, and said, "The only thing that people care about is the wallet: what goes in the wallet, what goes out of the wallet. That's what's important." Later that day, Reagan got back to focusing on the economy at a news conference.

To many opinion leaders in Washington, D.C., or New York City, Rhodes seemed like an uneducated rube. In fact, he did not like those types of "sophisticated" people either. Print journalists would clean up what he said, polish it, and make it intelligible. I produced several videos for Rhodes. They were difficult to edit because Rhodes's style was not of a television era. He would really do badly in today's world where people have cellphone video. His syntax and the way he'd put words together seemed rather crude and unusual.

But Rhodes had this gut feeling about what mattered to Ohio voters.

A Huckster to the End

Abe Zaidan

I covered Ohio governor Jim Rhodes for years, from when he was mayor of Columbus, Ohio in the 1960s to his last campaign for governor in 1986.

Rhodes was basically a huckster—a salesman with a gift for not answering questions and mangling the English language. He was always friendly to me—much friendlier to me than I was to him.

One time I walked into one of his news conferences with all these national reporters. He stopped the press conference as I walked in the door at the far end of the room.

He waved at me and said, "Wait a minute, there is Doctor Zaidan. Welcome Doctor Zaidan!"

I said, "Right, right."

Then he started asking me all these silly questions—it was his teasing style.

"What are you doing this afternoon?"

"I'm here to work."

"Do you want to play golf?"

"No, I don't want to play golf."

"Oh—you want to go bowling?"

But there was method to that madness because it was sort of a bridge to me and other journalists. It was also a disguise for him.

Another time I had just gotten back from covering the Republican National Convention when a neighbor asked if I had seen what Rhodes had written about me in my own newspaper, the *Akron Beacon Journal.*

I got a copy, and there was a column by James A. Rhodes. It was all about me, all tongue-in-cheek stuff.

"Abe Zaidan arrived at one of my press conferences with a pipe, shorts, golf clubs, and baseball gloves," Rhodes wrote, "He was really living it up here at the national convention."

"Abe said, 'Governor, I've had enough, you cover the convention for me.'"

The rest of the column was him covering me, such as:

"Abe went into a meeting here, and people asked, 'Who are you?'"

"Abe Zaidan."

"Get out of here—you don't even look like Abe Zaidan."

It was a funny, funny column.

He gave me a picture of himself at the peak of his career, and he wrote down on the corner, "To the esteemed reporter and political writer, Abe Zaidan."

What other governor would do that after you just slammed him, day in and day out?

I used to call him at midnight—because he was always home at midnight on the phone calling contributors. The last time I spoke to him, he was retired.

I said, "So what are you doing these days, Jim?"

He said he was selling air conditioners.

"Do you need to buy one?" he asked.

That's the way the conversation went—a huckster to the end.

Contrasting Governors

Lee Leonard

When I first met Governor James Rhodes during his second term in the late 1960s, I knew about the *Life* magazine scandal—allegations of misconduct involving Rhodes's pardon of a convicted mobster. But Rhodes seemed a father figure, an affable, down-to-earth guy. It was only later that I realized how hard it was going to be to cover him because he feasted on foiling reporters.

Rhodes didn't have a strong political philosophy. He had a "Jim Rhodes philosophy," and he knew that it worked for him. He talked about what he thought the people wanted to hear. He had a genuine feeling of the down-and-out, based on his humble background in southern Ohio. Rhodes was a middle-of-the-road, moderate Republican.

Rhodes was not a micromanager when it came to state government. He appointed the people that he wanted to do these jobs—and then let them do their jobs. Then he was free to see the big picture. Rhodes would meet with his cabinet, and after a few minutes he'd say, "Okay, I got to go. You take care of it." If an appointee got into trouble for doing something wrong, Rhodes was right on top of it. He'd say, "We're going to get to the bottom of this." He'd trust his people to go on their own and hoped they did the right thing. Usually, they measured up to that trust.

But Rhodes never built a farm team for the Republicans. He basically knew what was good for Jim Rhodes, and that is what he did. Undercover, he would encourage young Republicans that he liked to run for this and that office. But as far as standing out there with his arm around them and bestowing a blessing upon them—he just didn't do that. After he was term-limited out of office, the Democrats took over state government.

Governor John Gilligan was a big contrast to Rhodes. I didn't know him before he ran for governor against Auditor Roger Cloud in 1970 because he was a congressman, and I didn't cover Congress. I covered the campaign, and it was a big win for the Democrats. One reason was that the Republicans were caught in the Crofters scandal, involving allegations of bribery in a state loan program.

I still remember that first day when the transfer of power occurred. Rhodes had left office and Gilligan was in the inner governor's office. He got into that chair, leaned back, and said, "Ah, the first day of the new creation."

Gilligan had a wry sense of humor. He was genuinely funny—if you didn't take offense. His humor wasn't appreciated by a lot of people because it seemed snide, especially in print. It was like the day at the fairground for a simple photo opportunity: he took clippers to the sheep; he looked up at the photo and grinned saying, "I shear taxpayers, not sheep." It was a genuinely funny line, but it came back to haunt him when the Republicans used it against him.

Gilligan was very smart, very well-read, and brilliant. He had a clear liberal political philosophy and a deep compassion for people. I saw that side of him when we were riding from one event to another in the car. He talked about the mentally ill, and I distinctly remember how passionate he was.

Gilligan had a big agenda and accomplished most of it. The most controversial part was a state income tax increase, which helped pay for new programs. He had help from the legislature, especially after the Democrats took over in 1972. But Gilligan never courted legislators, and when he talked to legislators, it was to browbeat them. I'll always remember Democratic state representative Barney Quilter saying, "I got more time with Rhodes than I ever got with Gilligan."

On the surface, Gilligan's prospects for reelection in 1974 looked pretty good. He had done a lot. It was a bad year for the Republicans because of Watergate, plus Jim Rhodes was trying to make an unlikely comeback for governor. In fact, Rhodes had to get the state Supreme Court to decide that the two-term limit for governor was two *consecutive* terms, not two terms *total*. But Gilligan didn't understand how he was perceived by the public. People said, "Yeah, we know his brand, but this guy we just don't get." Gilligan lost to Rhodes's folksy style by a very small margin.

The other thing about Gilligan was that as the years went by, he and his former staff held reunions where they listed a litany of all the big things that happened during the Gilligan administration. It is a testament to his enduring success that when Rhodes came back as governor, he never sought to repeal or lower the income tax, and he didn't change many of the programs.

Rhodes said, "Never take the punching bag out of the gym." The Democrats were the punching bag—he let them do the unpopular things, and then he took credit for good results.

Good Old Boys and Brash New Guys
Mary Anne Sharkey

When I was assigned as a reporter to cover the Statehouse in Columbus, Ohio, the historic Neil House Hotel was where the good old boys, both legislators and lobbyists, hung out. It was a stunning period hotel and restaurant that once was the site of President William McKinley's home as well as the infamous meeting between California governor Ronald Reagan and Ohio governor James Rhodes, when Rhodes profanely told Reagan he was screwing up in his run for president.

There was a small section in the back of the hotel bar named the "Press Club." It was a private club where Vern Riffe, the powerful Speaker of the Ohio House of Representatives, liked to drink and swap stories. It was separated from the rest of the bar, where he enjoyed a bit of privacy. He had a small booth where he sat sipping cocktails with his usual stable of guys—legislators and lobbyists.

At first, it felt like a hostile environment for women. Certainly, in those days there were few women in state government or the press corps. And there was a lot of what was then called "womanizing." Male legislators would leave their wives at home and come to the big city—Columbus, the state capital—and cut up. About half of them had mistresses in Columbus or just fooled around.

But Vern was warm and friendly. If he saw me, he'd wave me over to sit down and have a drink with him. He joked that having a reporter at his table meant he could take a break from the lobbyists lined up to ask for favors. He was a great storyteller. I felt like I was taking a master class from Mr. Speaker, who was a great political strategist. He never took a note and had instant recall of everything people relayed to him.

Vern was a strong Speaker and didn't put up with a lot of nonsense. At that time, the legislators' offices were arranged with a suite with two small offices and a little area for a secretary with a couch. There was talk of legislators doing things on the couch that they shouldn't have been doing. Vern solved the problem: he took out the couches.

The Democrats were in power in the House of Representatives, but Vern was smart enough to know that he needed a cooperative Republican caucus. He would not only tell lobbyists how much money to give to his caucus, but he'd tell them how much money to give to Republicans, and to their leader Corwin Nixon, who was one of Vern's best friends. Modern-day speakers have diminished their ability to get things done by being so partisan. Vern always knew how many Republican votes he could count on, so he didn't have to bend to the troublemakers in his caucus, known as the "Young Turks." Future Speakers failed to follow his lead on working with the other party and thus lessened their own power.

Sherrod Brown was one these brash young guys. He was on the outs with Vern because he had a loud mouth. Vern would tell these kids to shut up, sit down, and learn a few things. But Sherrod wasn't willing to shut up. He was always on his feet giving a speech in the House of Representatives—just like John Kasich was over in the Ohio Senate. John Kasich walked into the Senate and undoubtedly gave a speech his first day.

One time I ran into Vern and Sherrod in the lobby of a Cleveland hotel where they were attending a political event. Vern walked up to Sherrod, who was running for Ohio secretary of state, and said, "Sherrod, you are a shit, you've always been a shit, and you'll always be a shit, but I'm going to support you anyway." Vern said it with a straight face, you know—not with a smile on his face. For once, Sherrod was speechless.

Another one of the new guys was Dick Celeste. I was very impressed with him—you couldn't help but be impressed. He was very smart and a mesmerizing speaker. He was elected as lieutenant governor when the office was elected separately from the governor. In that year, Republican Jim Rhodes was also elected governor, making a comeback for his third four-year term. Celeste and Rhodes developed a regular rivalry that lasted for a dozen years.

Celeste was planning to run against Rhodes in 1978. I think the press corps was so weary of Rhodes's bumbling ways, his being so inarticulate, and his lack of interest in issues. They were unabashedly pro-Celeste. No one wanted to cover Rhodes again. It kind of had a boomerang effect because there were people also inside the press corps who were saying things like, "It's not really our job to pick governors." In those days, the press was not supposed to have opinions, and there was supposed to be some semblance of objectivity. Celeste did run against Rhodes in 1978, and despite the favorable press coverage, he lost to Rhodes. Celeste went on to become governor in 1982 and walloped Rhodes's final attempted comeback in 1986.

There was talk that Celeste wanted to recruit Vern Riffe to run as his lieutenant governor in 1982. When Riffe asked me what I thought, I responded, "Do you really want to report to Jan Allen?" [one of Celeste's top staffers]. He roared with laughter and said, "Now that you put it that way, no."

Speaker Riffe did not want to take a demotion.

Ohio Characters

Tom Diemer

There were a lot of characters among the Ohio state legislators I covered, especially back in the 1970s.

Arthur Wilkowski was a state legislator from Toledo. He had a lisp—not just a lisp, but a spray—and was regarded as a great orator. He was from the north side of Toledo, a heavily Polish community in those days, which for some reason was called "Duketown." Art's political headquarters was a neighborhood bar called Jim and Lou's. He came down to Columbus with other urban Democrats from northern Ohio, like Vern Cook from Akron and Pat Sweeney from Cleveland.

These guys were different from the cornstalk brigade rural legislators who were chewing tobacco and walking around in suspenders and spats. Instead, they were smoking cigarettes, drinking beer, strolling around in loud ties and sport jackets. They were pro-union, bread-and-butter liberals, just trying to figure out how to operate in Columbus.

The first time I became aware of Art Wilkowski was when he helped engineer a quiet coup to replace A. G. Lancione as Speaker of the Ohio House of Representatives with Vern Riffe. They thought Lancione's time had come and passed—he was a nice guy but not the right guy. The Democrats had just taken over the majority in the legislature. I wanted to keep an eye on Art because his engine was always running.

Unfortunately, his career got derailed, pun intended, by his fixation with trains. He became obsessed with the idea of building a high-speed train line in Ohio. He got deeper and deeper into that issue to the exclusion of almost everything else. I thought he really lost his effectiveness. The cost of the project was enormous. Wilkowski wanted to build new right-of-ways. It wasn't a matter of adding an extra line, he wanted to build new rail lines, like the Japanese or French rail systems.

Another state legislator from Toledo was Marigene Valiquette, one of the few women in the legislature. She always wore a red carnation. When she campaigned for election, she had billboards that would say, "Vote for the *girl* with the red carnation." Talk about a different time.

She was cantankerous and difficult, smart but flaky, kind of good-looking but often a mess—lipstick smeared around and stuff. She was single. There were no rumors about her love life, or anything like that at all that I was privy to—not that those topics ever came up in those days. She was very effective, serving as chair of the finance committee of the state senate. She got a lot of stuff done and pissed a lot of people off.

I remember one time catching her around St. Patrick's Day at an event put on by a committee called the "Irish Northern Aid Committee." I understood enough about it to know that the group was an American front group, if not for the IRA, then certainly for Sinn Fein, the political arm of the IRA. In other words, it was a group that you might want to keep at arm's length if you were a conventional politician because there will always be rumors about gunrunning and stuff.

I said to her, "Gee, I'm kind of surprised to see you here."

She said, "Well, why? Why would you say that?"

"Well, you know this is a very sensitive political thing, given who these people are, some have linked them to the IRA."

"You wouldn't be asking me this question if you had an Irish mother."

I didn't know she had an Irish mother, given her last name. In fact, I do have an Irish mother too, but she didn't know that because my last name sounds German.

It just cracked me up because I had never thought of her as an ethnic politician.

From over in Youngstown, there was Tom Carney. There were two legislators by that name, "Big Tom" and "Little Tom." Big Tom was a state senator, a big fat guy with a buzz cut and blonde hair. He was a moderate to mildly conservative Democrat who had worked in steel mills. In fact, I think when he was first elected to the state senate, he was still working. He was with the United Steel Workers.

In the aftermath of the steel collapse in Youngstown, Governor Rhodes, Senator Carney, and other Youngstown politicians decided to tour the abandoned steel mill. There were these huge, scary hulks of the blast furnaces and these factories with smudged windows. There was nothing moving. We would drive right into the factory grounds and the open areas and gape at this stuff. The idea was, what can we do with this? How can we make lemonade out of these lemons?

So, I'm looking over at Carney, and I can see this sort of wistful look on his face as he's looking around. I thought, "It's good quote time." So, I sidled up to him and said, "Tom, this must be getting to you. You're probably seeing places that you worked, and there's nobody here now, you must be having a lot running through your head now."

He looked over at me, paused, and said, "No shit."

Classic midwestern answer. But I couldn't use the quote.

Intimidating Speaker

Bill Cohen

Vern Riffe, the legendary speaker of the Ohio House of Representatives, was a very intimidating man. For two decades, he ruled the House with an iron fist. Legislators who didn't do what he wanted were stripped of their committee assignments, and their bills didn't go anywhere. His main tools were money and access.

The Speaker had an annual birthday party for himself, a fundraiser where all the lobbyists came and bought tickets. If you were a lobbyist, then you made sure that he saw you there and that you shook his hand and said, "Happy Birthday Mr. Speaker." He'd look you in the eye and say, "Thank you, partner." Riffe kept track of how many tickets you bought, and if you didn't buy any tickets, then your bills didn't go anywhere. If you did buy tickets, there was no guarantee that your bills would go anywhere, but at least they wouldn't end up in the trash can.

On issues, Speaker Riffe was a moderate Democrat, certainly by today's standards. In those days, you also had Governor Jim Rhodes, who some liberals hated, but he was pretty moderate too. So, these people could work together: Rhodes and Riffe, and the other political leaders of that era. They were always mushing to the middle on issues and legislation.

We would say, "If Vern Riffe had been born in Upper Arlington, Ohio, then he would have run as a Republican. Instead, he was born in Scioto County, Ohio, and there it made more sense for him to run as a Democrat." But his policies wouldn't have been that much different.

In my dealings with Riffe, I found him very intimidating because of how he controlled access.

One time after the secession was over, Riffe came off the podium and into the hallway, where reporters were gathered. I'm the only radio guy there with the newspaper guys. I've got my microphone in there, and people are asking, "What's going on tomorrow?"

Suddenly, Riffe looks at me and says, "Who gave you permission to turn on that microphone and tape recorder?"

I was stunned. I was just doing my job like I always did. Ironically, the state of Ohio helped to pay for these news reports for public radio. Of course, I didn't turn my tape recorder off. I just held the mike there, and we moved on.

Heck, I was just a small potato, nobody special, a little fly buzzing around annoying Riffe. So, I can imagine what he was like with the real players when he used his muscle to bargain with them.

I know that people will often say, "Oh things were much better when Speaker Riffe was here: the trains ran in time, bills got passed, and things got resolved quickly."

My response: sure, but that's not democracy; that's not free speech; that's not free debate.

We will never have another Speaker Riffe in Ohio because no one will ever be allowed to stay in one office that long, accumulating power.

Double Disappointment
Paul Tipps

One day Speaker Vern Riffe went down to see Governor Jim Rhodes, with whom he had a good relationship.

Riffe said, "Governor, I really need a favor."

Rhodes said, "Well, what is it?"

Riffe said, "As you know, there is a member of the racing commission I'd like you to appoint as the commission's president." And the Speaker talked a little about the person.

Rhodes replied, "I am really sorry, but I can't do that."

Riffe was stunned, and he didn't say a word.

Then Rhodes said, "But he is a good guy. I'll appoint him to the next vacancy that comes open."

"But remember," the governor continued, "If I appoint him, then he is my guy."

The Speaker was doubly disappointed.

A Rhodes Guy

Bob Ney

I was looking for a job in 1979, and somebody said, well, you campaigned for Governor Rhodes as a college student, and maybe he can help.

So, I went to see Roy Martin, who was *the* chief of staff for Jim Rhodes. I mean, everything ran through Roy. I even knew a cabinet member who got his college roommate's son a janitor job, and when Roy found out that it didn't go through him, he made the cabinet member fire the kid. So, it was *the* Roy Martin. Martin always scared me. When I was a state representative, he always scared me.

Roy was not a conversationalist.

When I went in, he looked at me over his glasses, and said, "Yes?"

I said, "Well, Mr. Martin, I'm looking for a job." I explained my situation.

He handed me a Department of Administrative Services application, and said, "Here, on the back of this application, there's three lines for references. On one of the lines, put 'James A. Rhodes' as one of the references. Okay, goodbye."

So, I went over and filed the application with Webb Davis at the Department of Administrative Services.

About six or seven weeks later, I hadn't heard anything, so I went back to see Mr. Martin.

"What's going on?" he asked.

"Well, really don't want to bother you, Mr. Martin, but I don't have a job."

"Why not?"

"I don't know, Mr. Martin."

"Did you put 'James A. Rhodes' on the back of the application?"

"Yes, sir."

"Step out, please."

I stepped out.

They buzzed me back in, and Martin said, "Go over at 1:30 p.m. today and see Phil Hamilton, Department of Administrative Services. You know who that is? Go see him."

Well, at 1:30 p.m., I go into Phil Hamilton's office. He is sitting there with Webb Davis, who is not looking happy.

"Webb, what about that job application?" asked Hamilton.

Webb mumbles that I wasn't qualified for that job, and on and on and on...

Mr. Hamilton rolled his chair around as if I wasn't even there. He looked at Webb and said, "This man worked for Governor Rhodes in 1974. The back of his application had 'James A. Rhodes' as a reference."

"Now Webb, I don't care if you find, create, or shit a job for him, he's to have a job."

At 3:30 p.m., I got a phone call, and they said I was the head of education and healthcare for the Ohio Office of Appalachia. Webb Davis never forgave me.

Fair and Evenhanded

Jerry Austin

This story is about a county party chair who was a total, complete pro.

In 1976, a state senator in Ohio named Don Pease was elected to the U.S. Congress. And because he was halfway through the state senate seat term, the Democrats in the state senate would appoint someone to fill the seat for the remainder of the term. The Democratic Senate leader asked the chairman of the Democratic Party in the county where the district was located to nominate someone for the appointment.

The county chairman called a meeting of the executive committee and invited candidates seeking the appointment to address the committee. One was a city officeholder named Ron Nabokowsky, the second was the president of the city council, and the third was a local lawyer.

After the presentation, the county chairman sent a letter to the Democratic senate leader: "We have three excellent candidates for this position. We leave it up to you to choose whichever of the three candidates you think would be best to serve." He sent each of the candidates a copy of the letter.

But on the original letter to the Democratic Senate leader, he circled the name Nabokowsky.

Nabokowsky was appointed.

Changing of the Guard
Lee Leonard

I first met Dick Celeste when he came into the Ohio House of Representatives in 1971—the fateful year when the state income tax increase was enacted by Governor Gilligan. He was one of several new Democrats from Cleveland and part of the younger generation. Celeste stood out in this new group; there's no question about it. Not only was he physically prominent—he was a tall guy, vigorous and youthful—he was thoughtful and dynamic.

I remember going to dinner with just him at one of the hotel dining rooms. We had a good private conversation. He was impressive. With Celeste, it was more than saying, "Oh this guy is going to go somewhere." It was watching how he related to people and the things he was doing. Some of the legislators would just come in and sit in their chairs, and say "yes" and "no," maybe jabber a bit. But there were others that worked on their own projects, were not afraid of hard work, and did things behind the scenes. You could see that Celeste was a guy on the move.

Celeste quickly moved up in the legislature. He was named the chair of the Cuyahoga County delegation in his second term and then rose in the Democratic leadership. Then in 1974 he ran for lieutenant governor, saying he would be Governor Gilligan's strong right-hand man. Celeste won, but Gilligan lost. Republican governor Jim Rhodes didn't have much use for Celeste, but Celeste kept busy getting ready to run against Rhodes in 1978.

During his second eight years as governor, Rhodes was on autopilot because in his first eight years he had accomplished almost everything he wanted to do. So, in the first couple of years of his third term, he just sparred with the Democrats who had control of the state legislature. After that, they all decided to work together. But there wasn't really anything great accomplished in those years. They just kept the state afloat.

Rhodes's biggest effort was four bond issues in 1975 to finance new state programs. Celeste was the appointed Democratic leader to campaign against the bond issues, which were defeated soundly. Ironically, all those proposals were eventually accomplished, just not while Rhodes was in office. When Celeste ran against Rhodes for governor in 1978, Celeste proposed tax increases to address public education. Rhodes came back with his standard "no new taxes" response. But then Rhodes had to raise taxes eventually himself to pay for the budget.

It was close—a hard-fought campaign. Rhodes was legendary in that he would get up early and campaign all day, every day. Dick Celeste was one of the hardest working campaigners that I ever saw. It made me laugh when Rhodes said of Celeste, "Oh, he couldn't be governor because he doesn't know the meaning of hard work." Well, Celeste could work every bit as hard as Rhodes. Rhodes was nevertheless reelected by a small margin.

Celeste was of out of Ohio for most of Rhodes's final term as governor, serving as the director of the Peace Corps. But he was back in the state in 1982 and won the Democratic gubernatorial nomination over Ohio attorney general Bill Brown. It was the was the first time that I was fooled on election night. I was responsible for calling the election for United Press International. As I remember, Celeste took about a two percent lead—and that held all night long. I was thinking, "Something is going to happen, and Billy is going to come out from under, and he's going to snatch it at the last minute." Well, it didn't happen that way. I was being pounded on by our Washington bureau, saying "Call it, call it!" I knew from past elections how people had gotten in trouble by calling it too early. I had been right on the Gilligan-Rhodes race in 1974, but on this one I was not right. Celeste held his lead and won by a small margin. Basically, he campaigned to be "governor from Cleveland," and it worked.

In the general election, Celeste faced Republican Congressman Bud Brown, and we all knew there wasn't going to be any contest because Brown had spent so much time away from Ohio in Congress. He didn't know the state, and he didn't have the drive and ambition to run an effective statewide campaign. He was a smart guy, but he was not the right guy to be running for governor.

When Celeste ran for reelection in 1986, his opponent was Jim Rhodes, who trying to make one more comeback. It wasn't a real contest: Celeste was as energetic as ever, but Rhodes was past his prime.

Rhodes tried to make an issue of rumors about Celeste's marital infidelities, but reporters were not interested. There were different standards then. We would talk to politicians after hours and spend time with them in the Neil House. We would hear stories, but we wouldn't write about them because the stories were not part of the business we were covering. Today you hear all kinds of personal stories about legislators and public officials because it's considered fair game for reporters to write about such things. In those days, it wasn't considered fair game. If you heard an off-color story about Celeste, Riffe, or somebody else, you just left that alone.

Celeste was a successful governor, leaving his mark on Ohio. At heart, he was a 1960s liberal, a good bit like Gilligan, but more careful politically. Celeste campaigned as a "Rhodes scholar," having learned the art of telling people what they wanted to hear, and he governed as a "Rhodes liberal," making government as responsive to people as was politically possible. Celeste lacked management skills and made some poor judgments, but he got a lot done. He restored fiscal stability to the state budget, modestly expanded programs without expanding the state payroll, and appointed record numbers of minorities and women to state government. In his last term, he was a bit more liberal, calling again for a tax increase to fund education. He had presidential ambitions that ended when his infidelities finally became public. That story marked a major change in political coverage in Ohio and at the national level.

A Hell of a Good Story
Bill Hershey

Governor Dick Celeste was such a departure from Governor Jim Rhodes. He was well-spoken; he was big; he was handsome; he was charismatic—at least by Ohio standards. I wanted to be skeptical of him because I didn't think the other reporters were—many reporters were infatuated with Celeste. So, I tried to take a less adoring approach to him, but when he took over, I got a little bit seduced myself because he was a very active governor.

Celeste wanted to get things done, and I wrote a story comparing him to the Woody Hayes football approach: three yards and a cloud of dust. He was a whirling dervish of a governor. The Ohio economy was in shambles when he took over in 1983. At that time there were thousands of people working in the steel mills, rubber shops, and the auto-parts factories in Ohio's cities, and those jobs were imperiled. Celeste had a lot of new policy ideas—like the Thomas Edison vocational programs—ideas that you could really bite into as a reporter. I covered Celeste's first budget and his so-called "90 percent" tax increase. It was an exciting time in Ohio politics.

It was during the budget battle that I had one of the best experiences I've had as a reporter. Celeste's proposed budget, including the tax increase, easily passed the Ohio House of Representatives due to Speaker Vern Riffe and a large Democratic majority. But things were much tougher in the Ohio state senate, where the Democrats had just a one-seat majority over the Republicans, seventeen to sixteen. The Republicans were united in opposition to the tax increase, and the Democrats had their own problems. Their leader, Harry Meshel, was new as president of the Senate and untested, having led a coup against the long-serving leader, Oliver Ocasek, a couple of years before. Ocasek was from the Akron area and a very smart guy, but he could dwell on a disappointment like that. He was something of a self-righteous person who thought of himself a little bit above politics. And to add to the drama, he was out of pocket as the key vote approached.

Ocasek and his wife had been in a serious traffic accident in Florida, but nobody knew exactly where or what was going on. So, the *Akron Beacon Journal* sent me down to find out. It turned out he was in Hollywood, Florida, at his wife's side, who was in a coma because of the accident. Then on the day of the crucial vote, Ocasek flew back to Columbus. He was really hurting. He cast the seventeenth and deciding "yes" vote in a whisper. Afterwards Ocasek flew right back to be with his wife and did not talk to the press. But Celeste spoke with him and shared his gratitude with reporters.

It was a hell of a good story: front-page pictures of Ocasek coming off the airplane and on the Senate floor, doing his job under painful circumstances.

Little Did We Know
Tim Miller

In 1988, several Ohio reporters were covering the National Governors Association, and they allowed us to go to the closing dinner, putting us together in the back of the big pavilion.

We happened to be sitting with the reporters from Arkansas, and they were gushing about Dick Celeste, then governor of Ohio. They said, "This guy's going be the next president. He's so intelligent and has so much charisma."

A couple of the Ohio reporters said, "Well, your guy is pretty good, too." Arkansas governor Bill Clinton was being discussed as a leading candidate.

Then the Arkansas reporters say, "Well, there's no way our guy can get elected because he's got a woman problem."

We start laughing, "Well, we think our guy does too, but what's been written about your guy in Arkansas?"

He said, "Well, nothing's really been written in Arkansas."

We said, "Well, our guy has been a bit unluckier, but we're not sure it keeps him out of the race."

Little did we know how their infidelities would become part of public discussion and debate, first for Celeste, later for Clinton.

A Little Piece of History

Jim Underwood

After Dick Celeste was reelected as Ohio governor in 1986, there was a sense that his next step was to run for president of the United States. We thought he had the record for a plausible presidential campaign, but we also we had a sense that Dick wanted to run, and he wanted to do it right away. When the campaign of the front-runner for the Democratic presidential nomination, Colorado senator Gary Hart, collapsed because of an extramarital affair, there was talk that Celeste saw an opening to get into the presidential race.

I was having lunch with a colleague one day, and I said, "I just find it strange that Dick Celeste sees the exodus of Gary Hart from the campaign as an opportunity to launch his own campaign. He will face the same issue as Hart."

My colleague agreed, recalling many rumors about Celeste that were exacerbated a bit by the peculiar relationship between Dick and his wife Dagmar. It didn't seem rational to me. Why would Celeste put himself in that position to have to defend himself? The question would be: Did he have such a relationship, or didn't he?

But what got me focused on this story was a lunch I had with a woman who was leaving the Celeste administration. She had been a source for some of my stories, and it was my way of saying thanks.

Out of the blue, she said, "I'm so worried about Dick."

I said, "Why are you worried about Dick?"

She said, "Well, I just worry about him—I just worry who is going to take care of him."

I said, "He has lots of people around to take care of him."

She went on, "Not people that really care about him."

At this point, she started to cry.

It was one of those "holy shit" moments.

I leaned across the table and said, "Are you screwing this guy?"

Then the tears just started to pour down her face—we almost had to leave the restaurant.

So, I had one source, and about that time, Mary Ann Sharkey of the *Cleveland Plain Dealer* indicated to me that she had a source inside the administration—a single source—on the governor's behavior. But it wasn't clear if it was the same source as mine.

I had a candid conversation about it with Tim Miller of the *Dayton Daily News*, who was also looking into the rumors. I said, "We're playing under the same set of rules as you, except my editors are not going to let me pull the trigger on that story with a single source. I'm going to need at least two sources to do that."

My thinking was: "Let's just end this nonsense. Let's ask the guy straight up and see what he does with it. If there's a story, let's do the story ourselves and not give it away to the national reporters."

Then the governor held a routine press conference. I can't remember what it was about—I don't think anybody remembers what the hell that press conference was about.

Three of us were sitting there at the press conference—Tim Miller on my left and Mary Ann Sharkey on my right—and I said, "Which one of us is going to ask THE question?" We started joking about it, and they said they would give me a quarter if I asked THE question.

But on a serious note, Sharkey said, "Well, any of us that can get to ask a question should do it." The way it shook out, it ended up being me—it was just the luck of the draw that the opportunity came to me.

So, Deb Phillips, the press secretary, was about to end the press conference, and I said, "Wait a minute. I got a question."

Dick Celeste was starting to leave, and he turned back, with this big shit-eating grin on his face. He may have thought I was going to ask him a question couched in humorous terms, as I sometimes did.

Instead, I asked, "Is there anything in your personal life that would preclude you from being president, as it has Gary Hart?"

At that point, Celeste kind of canted his head to the left, the grin left his face, and he gave me that thousand-yard stare.

He said, "No."

I'm getting this shocked look from everybody in the room, like "I can't believe you asked that. What's wrong with you?"

Deb Phillips said, "Where did that come from?" I noticed she was doing eye contact with Celeste. They got him out of the room right away.

Sharkey and Miller started laughing, thinking back to our joking around before the news conference. Spontaneously, Sharkey reached over and put a quarter in my hand. It was just part of the joke, but it is THE thing everybody remembers about that press conference.

Afterwards Sharkey said, "I think we've got him."

I was upfront with my editors, "I'm working to find a second source on this story, but don't be surprised if the *Cleveland Plain Dealer* breaks this story before we do."

My editors said, "We will go with the story if we've got the story. But if we don't have the story, let somebody else pull the trigger."

When the *Plain Dealer* broke the story a week or so later, we did our own story based on theirs.

Well, that was a little piece of history. A lot of people took the question to mean that I didn't like Dick Celeste. Nothing could be further from the truth. To this day, there are few people that I admire more than Dick Celeste. It was the question that any reporter would have asked him given the opportunity.

A Little Clarity
Mary Anne Sharkey

The front-runner for the 1988 Democratic nomination, Colorado senator Gary Hart, dropped out because of allegations of womanizing on a boat appropriately named *Monkey Business*. That gave Ohio governor Dick Celeste an opening to run, and soon after, he formally announced his interest in the campaign.

I got a call from my *Cleveland Plain Dealer* colleague Brent Larkin.

Brent said, "Are you thinking what I'm thinking?"

I said, "You mean about Celeste getting into the race because Gary Hart had to get out of the race? And Celeste having the same problem?"

Brent responded, "Yeah, exactly."

I said, "Brent, I am thinking about that. But I don't think our editors would ever run a story about Celeste's womanizing. I really don't."

Brent said, "What if we could verify it?"

I said, "I don't think verification is going to be very difficult, to be honest with you. Frankly, I know of a couple of women who have had affairs with him."

He said, "Do you think we should go back and talk with these people or what?"

I said, "Brent, sure, but you better talk to the editors first. I don't think they'll ever run this story, and if they do, they're not going to name anyone. So, what's the point?"

At the time, I didn't know that the editors were upset with Celeste and more open to a critical story.

So, Brent and I went back and forth. It was not clear what to do. We decided to investigate some more.

Debbie Phillips, the governor's press secretary, got wind of the fact that Brent and I were talking to people about the sensitive topic. So, she and I went out and had drinks. I verified to her that we were looking into the story, but I told her I didn't think the editors would run it.

So, Celeste knew we were interested in the issue. He shouldn't have been surprised when it came up, and he should have been prepared to handle it. All he needed to say was, "None of your business. This is my private life." That would have been the end of it.

Here is the way it rolled out. The governor held a routine press conference. It was in the cabinet room, and the press corps wasn't very interested in the topic, whatever it was.

Before it started, I was joking with Jim Underwood of the Horvitz papers and Tim Miller of the *Dayton Daily News* about who would ask Celeste about his own Hart-like behavior. As a joke, we offered Jim a quarter to ask THE question.

At the end of the press conference, Jim did get a chance to ask a question, and he asked Celeste, "Is there anything in your personal life that would preclude you from being president as it has Gary Hart?" Celeste just looked at him and said, "No." Jim rephrased it, and again Celeste denied it and left the room. Jim was a quarter richer.

The press conference denial made it more than just a story about Celeste's mistresses. It was now a story about his lying too.

Our editors were fine with this kind of story—which got the womaning issue out in the open. But we still had to double check our sources. It took us about ten days to write the story.

It was on the front page of the paper, with the headline "Celeste Womanizing Worries Top Aides," with the subtitle "Links to three women may imperil presidential ambitions." The women were not named. Celeste announced he would not run for president a few days later, citing other reasons, but acknowledging that both public and private conduct were subject to press scrutiny.

Brent and I were less than happy with the newspaper's lawyers who got involved and took out most of the salient details about the women, including a governor's office intern and a couple of the other women on the state or campaign payrolls. We felt they had gutted the story of the most important elements, namely, that Celeste was their boss, and they drew salaries from the taxpayers or campaign contributors. And, by the way, these three women were the only ones we could check and double check—there was a bigger roster.

Oddly, the story was one of my best-known stories, but something I wanted to forget because the real story had been gutted by timid lawyers.

A Moral Dilemma
Mike Curtin

Gene Jordan was an old-school character sent by central casting: a hard-smoking, hard-drinking, hard-cussing, hard-driving political writer. He wore his Republican politics on his sleeve, wrote the most biased stuff in the world, and was proud of it. He might have a thin veneer of objectivity occasionally, as a fig leaf, but he worked for a Republican newspaper, the *Columbus Dispatch*, and he was going to report the Republican version of events. Later there was an effort to reform the paper, and a new editor called Gene into this office and said, "Gene, the stuff you're writing is so biased, and it doesn't look good." Jordan replied, "You're the first person who ever told me I'm supposed to be fair."

The first and biggest moral dilemma I faced as a young journalist was trying to figure out whether and how to clean up after Gene Jordan. From time to time, I served as the acting night editor, and part of the job was to edit copy that came in during the night. Jordan would often cover political meetings and turn in a story late in the evening.

One night, I hear the elevator door open and some staggering steps coming down the hall. I look over, and sure enough, it's Gene Jordan as drunk as any human being could possibly be, shuffling into the newsroom. He tosses his coat aside, stumbles over to his typewriter—an old-style Underwood typewriter with copy paper—and starts banging out something. Then he nods off, then he wakes up, keeps typing, nods off and wakes up, and types some more. This goes on for a while. Then he takes the copy off his typewriter, weaves past my desk, drops his copy in the wire basket, and departs.

So, I pick up his copy and try to read it, but it's completely indecipherable. I couldn't tell if he'd been to a Democratic meeting, a Republican meeting, or a Libertarian meeting, I mean it was just all gibberish. I'm sure he thought it was eloquent prose, but in his drunken state, it was completely unintelligible.

Here I am, an acting night city editor only on the job for two years or so, and a legend, not only in Columbus but in the state of Ohio, had dropped in the basket copy that was just hieroglyphics.

What do I do? Do I just leave a note for the morning crew, the big bosses, that here's what Gene Jordan turned in, which would basically be to throw him under the bus? I mean everyone knew he was a drinker, but this copy couldn't be published because you couldn't tell what it was.

I decided the last thing in the world I'm going to do is throw Gene Jordan under the bus.

So, I started making phone calls to find out where Jordan had been that evening. I started going through the city desk rolodex of political contacts to see what meetings were taking place in Columbus that evening. After making a few phone calls, I found out where Jordan was likely to have been. Next, I started making phone calls to people who were there and could tell me what happened. Then I rewrote the story completely from start to finish. The story was published the next day under Gene Jordan's byline.

I never heard a word from Gene, never an acknowledgment, never a "thank you."

Just Instinct

Jerry Austin

In 1986, Anthony Celebrezze ran for Ohio attorney general. He didn't have any primary opposition, so I suggested to him that he spend time in a Cleveland city police patrol car to get the understanding of what police go through during a shift. So, he arranged to ride a shift from midnight to eight in the morning with two Cleveland police officers.

The next day I called him to ask how it went. He said, "We got into a chase, and we're chasing this car. It stopped and the driver ran. The police officers ran after the driver, and I ran with them."

I said, "You ran with them?"

He said, "Yeah, I ran with them, and I tackled the guy, then they arrested him."

I said, "Tony, what were you, crazy?"

He said, "It was just instinct."

I recreated that spot and used it in the campaign.

We won the race easily.

Like Twins

Bob Ney

An interesting thing about the legendary Ohio congressman Wayne Hays was that his full name was Wayne Levere Hays. And it's on his tombstone: Wayne Levere Hays. He used to say, "Do you know who I am? I'm Wayne Levere Hays." That's what he would do.

We were sort of like political twins. Wayne Hays was a graduate of Ohio State University with a teaching degree, and so was I. Wayne Hays and I were both from Belmont County, Ohio. Wayne Hays's first government position was on the school board of the City of Flushing; my first government position was safety director for the City of Bellaire. Wayne Hays was a state senator and a state representative, and I was a state senator and a state representative as well. Wayne Hays was elected to Congress and became the chairman of the House Administration Committee, and I was too. Wayne Hays resigned from Congress due to a sex scandal, and I resigned due to a political scandal. We just crossed each other's paths in so many ways. I was always a big Wayne Hays fan, even though I ran against him.

When I was raised in Belmont County, like every other kid, we knew about the House Administration Committee and its long-serving chairman Wayne Hays. The chairman of the House Administration Committee was appointed by the Speaker of the U.S. House of Representatives. When I came to the Congress, I wanted to be on that committee to help the Speaker run the House of Representatives. The committee oversees the operations of the House, from offices to staff to the Capitol Police—and elections as well—all the sorts of things the members of Congress care a lot about on a day-to-day basis.

Of course, I also knew about the power of the House Administration Committee and what it could do from my district—and that was from Wayne Hays. If you were in Congress, you could call Wayne Hays, and he would get stuff done for you. You needed a roll of toilet paper, and he'd make sure one was delivered to your house. I mean the guy was amazing. The members needed to mail out their newsletters, and Wayne made it happen. You needed new carpet? You wanted your walls painted? You requested new computer equipment? Wayne was the guy, not to mention parking spaces. He was very tough and collected a lot of favors, the best currency in politics.

So, chairing the House Administration Committee was in my political DNA. How I got to that position is a long story, and it begins with Wayne Hays.

In 1980, I was about twenty-six years old and thinking about running against Wayne Hays, who was then back in Ohio, serving in the Ohio House of Representatives.

Some people said, "Wayne Hays won that election even after he resigned due to a sex scandal with Elizabeth Ray. He can't be beat."

I said, "Of course, everybody likes Mr. Hays, but I could beat him."

"But you're a Republican, there's no Republicans down there in Belmont County."

"Yeah, I know, but I could beat him."

So, I quit my state job, moved back to Belmont County, and filed against Wayne Hays.

George Contos, who had lost to Hays two years prior, warned me it would be a tough campaign.

He said, "Look, I was out there campaigning. I had a hot dog in one hand, a Coca-Cola in the other, and an older guy, eighty-something years old, walked up and said, 'What's your name?' I told him and he said, 'You're running against Wayne Hays?' I said 'Yes.' And the guy punched me square in the face, and Coke flew all over me."

When I was out campaigning, I looked carefully at every old man that came toward me. Finally, one old guy came up and said, "Who are you?" I told him, "Bob Ney, I'm from Bellaire and running against Wayne Hays." He said, "Well, that's in Belmont County where Mr. Hays is from. I hear it is a very tough place." So, I felt more comfortable out campaigning.

Hays and I debated each other maybe twelve times that whole campaign. Wayne could pick a lock with his tongue. I mean the guy was a debater from his Ohio State days, very articulate, and very aggressive.

Our first debate was in that fire hall, and it was packed, the doors were open, people inside and outside. The county commissioner candidates and all the local officeholders were there.

I went first because Hays was the incumbent. I said, "My name is Bob Ney, and I'm from Bellaire, Ohio. I'm the city safety director. I've done a job down there, and I want to do a job for you in Columbus, Ohio. I'm going to stand up for coal."

"Now, there's two bottom lines here," I said, and like Governor Jim Rhodes, I pulled out my wallet, and said, "Mr. Hays can tell you things, I can tell you things. But the issue of the election is this wallet. The money that the taxpayers put in and the money the government tries to take out. I want to make your wallet better for you, so you can use your money for your families."

Then I said: "There's another thing, too. I'm about to make a statement you're not going to like. I am proud to not be a Democrat standing here today." And I mean you could hear moans, like a wave going through the crowd like "O-H-I-O" at a ball game.

"Now, my parents are Democrats, my great-grandfather was a member of the Democratic committee here. Democrats are wonderful people. But I am proud to not be a Democrat because I know there's no elected Republicans in this county. I can't come back to you two years later, like Mr. Hays is doing, and say 'Ah, I really can't tell you what I did.' Mr. Hays had a glorious career in Congress, I don't doubt that, but he hasn't done anything in the state. I'll have to come back and prove myself."

I sat down, and they applauded a lot.

Hays got up and said, "That boy isn't even from Belmont County. He's not from here. He's not from Bellaire. Jim Rhodes and those big oil bullies sent him down here."

Then he said, "I'm glad you're proud about proving stuff because you're never going to be in the state legislature to prove a damn thing."

They applauded a lot, too.

I barely beat Hays, by a thousand or so votes. Vern Riffe, the Speaker of the Ohio House of Representatives and the leader of the Democrats, didn't think I could win the race. But Hays was making comments about Vern about how he might run for Speaker himself against Vern someday. So, when I won, Vern privately told me he didn't mind too much losing the seat. Members of both parties welcomed me, although some Wayne Hays addicts told me "We're taking you out in two years. You're history in two years."

Two years later, I'm running for reelection. I'm on top of the world, my poll numbers are out the ceiling, and I was pretty popular. I was the first freshman to be on the secretary of finance committee. The Republicans put me on good committees because my district was so bad—it was so Democratic. But the Democrats wanted that seat back—the Republicans were just six seats short of flipping Vern out as Speaker. Well, Vern aggressively sought to keep the House safe for himself.

I was told that Vern's guys told him, "Ney is losing his race."

Vern said, "Well, who the hell is running against him?"

They said, "A guy named Jack Cera. We wouldn't give him any money."

Vern said, "Well damn, we better write him a check."

I lost to Cera by 126 votes.

But Vern was nice to me as I was leaving the House and when I came back to the Ohio state senate in 1984.

That's What's Fair
Bob Ney

I was appointed to the Ohio Senate in 1984, and I loved working in the Ohio Senate for the ten years I was there. I served on, and eventually chaired, the Senate finance committee. We funded the state senate's budget, the governor's budget, the secretary of state's budget, the parks and, you know, everything else. I liked the workings on how things actually worked—I liked that a lot.

I've always said this in politics: if you want to know something, all you have to do is walk in the front desk of most offices, and say, "Hi, how are you?" And that's how I could find out almost anything.

One time, my Senate page was graduating from Ohio State, and she was friends with Representative Marc Guthrie's page, and found out that he was going to stack the finance committee hearing room with a bunch of people. Marc had a bill before my committee, and he was lining up people to come in there and pack the committee room that night—just pack it and protest everything. Marc was doing this because he wanted this mandated benefits bill that I didn't want. So, I simply recessed the committee, and I thought that was that.

Well, Marc went ballistic and somehow convinced Vern Riffe, the Speaker of the House, that I had done something against him, like holding up a piece of legislation that Vern wanted.

Meanwhile, I had an emergency bill set up with suspension of the rules, and it was all wired for quick passage. Then suddenly it just came to a halt over in the House—my bill just died.

So, I made an appointment to go see Speaker Riffe. I went over to his office. He had a grandfather clock, and the pendulum would swing, a minute at a time, you know, back and forth. When Vern liked you, he called you "partner." If he didn't like you, he didn't call you "partner." No "partner" this time.

Vern said: "Well, you know, I'm told that you did this thing to screw up my bill." But I didn't do anything to screw the legislation he wanted from the finance committee. It might have been Stan Aronoff, the Republican president of the Senate, or somebody else. Vern and I were friends.

All of a sudden, I looked at Vern, and I said; "You're not fair."

Then he launched into a tirade. I watched the clock pendulum go back and forth to just get myself through with this explosion by Vern.

"Who are you to say, 'you're not fair?'" he shouted, "You do what you do, I'll do what I do, and that's what's fair."

This meeting was done, and I left. I went over and bitched to Aronoff. I said, "Something's going on. You guys are all doing something!"

About a day later, Vern's top staffer, Tom Winters, comes to the back of the floor of the Senate. They call me back, I leave the floor of the Senate, and I go back to see Tom.

I said, "How are you?"

Tom said, "Fine. The Speaker says hello, your bill is going to be voted on in the next hour on the floor of the House."

The Speaker had found out the truth. That's how Vern was.

Nobody Serious

Joanne Limbach

In 1976, I decided to run for Tuscarawas County Commissioner.

I had been elected to the school board in 1971, volunteered on campaigns, and developed a good relationship with the local Democratic Party chairman. He was a curmudgeon, the kind of long-serving, small-county chairman that was common in Ohio those days. He also encouraged me to try things politically.

One of the incumbent Commissioners could not decide whether he wanted to run again. So, I decided to help him along by taking out petitions to run for his seat.

Then the commissioner said that he thought he was being "railroaded" out of office. I went over to the local newspaper—that's when you could easily meet with the editors. It was fun: I had an engineer's hat on and a railroad whistle. I told the editor that it was certainly untrue that I was trying to railroad the commissioner out of office. It was just that the commissioner needed to make up his mind. In the end, he decided to not seek reelection.

One night I was working at Democratic headquarters when I overheard a conversation between the chairman and another guy about the open seat for county commissioner.

"You know," the guy said, "if nobody serious gets into this county commissioner race, I'm going to throw my hat in."

I said, "Hey, I'm in the race."

He said, "As I said, if nobody serious gets into the race."

The guy did get into the race, and "nobody serious" ended up winning.

I was the first woman elected as county commissioner in Tuscarawas County.

What's in a Name?

Jerry Austin

There's a legendary story in Ohio about a county party chairman from Vinton County, the smallest county in Ohio. It's so small that the radio station was in the dry-cleaning store. The country chairman's name was Red Mahaffey.

As the story goes, the executive director of the Ohio Democratic Party came out from Columbus to meet with Red. He drove up the road to his house, and all of a sudden, twenty or so dogs descended upon the car. The dogs kept barking and barking. The executive director was sitting in his car and didn't know what to do.

Finally, Red came up and said, "They're okay, they're okay, they won't bother you."

When the visitor got out of the car, he said, "Well, Red, how do you keep track of all the names of all these dogs? You must have twenty dogs here."

Red said, "Watch this. Here Trixie, here Trixie." All the dogs responded.

He had named them all Trixie.

A Great Mentor

Joanne Limbach

Dick Celeste promised to bring more women into state government, and when he was elected governor in 1982, he kept his pledge.

I had campaigned for him in 1974, 1978, and 1982 and was part of a group called the "card party" that Dick put together to advise him. When he was lieutenant governor, I headed his task force on women and did some other things. But I never thought I'd go to work in Columbus.

When Dick proposed appointing me as tax commissioner, the initial reaction was a general freak-out, "Who is this woman?"

I said to Dick, "You know, I'm not an accountant. I'm not an attorney." All of the previous tax commissioners had been accountants and attorneys, except for one, who had been a county auditor.

Dick said, "The best thing is that you know what you don't know. You surround yourself with good, smart people. You don't have to know about the technical aspects, you just have to understand the overall issues."

I had some things going for me: I was a woman, relatively young, and an elected official from a rural county, so I scored well on what today is called diversity.

I also had a great mentor in State Representative Bill Hinig. What mattered to Bill was that I was a constituent and had the new governor's confidence. He felt obligated to help me since I really didn't know anything about taxes. He took me everywhere with him and helped me climb a steep learning curve.

Hinig gave me an entrée into politics that I could not have gotten any other way. He introduced me to the "good old boys" network in Columbus, including Speaker of the Ohio House of Representatives, Vern Riffe. To Riffe, my credentials were being an elected county commissioner. He was fond of quoting Sam Rayburn, the great Speaker of the U.S. House of Representatives, who, when asked about John F. Kennedy's cabinet appointees, said that he would have been more comfortable if one of them had been an elected dog warden.

I'd have drinks with Bill, Vern, and their colleagues, listen to their stories, and learn from them. Bill and his friends were big band people, and they like to go out dancing. I would go along with others like state representatives Mary Boyle, a Democrat from Cleveland, and Marie Tansey, a Republican from Vermillion. One time Marie was talking about something political that had happened that day. She didn't know me, so she gave me a look. Bill said, "You can say anything in front of her that you would say in front of me. She's trustworthy." It was so wonderful to be part of that group. Some feminine folks were furious that I did this socializing—that was not quite acceptable in those days—but it gave me credibility.

In the official composite picture of the tax commissioners, you could tell me from the others because I was the only one with hair on my forehead!

Gray Government
Lee Leonard

I first met George Voinovich when he served in the Ohio state legislature. He was an anomaly, a Republican from Cuyahoga County. The Republican leader would let him go against the party and vote for things that were needed for his district—and to align with the people in the Cleveland area. He was an interesting legislator. Did I think that he would ever be governor at that time? No.

After a couple of years, Voinovich left the legislature to become Cuyahoga County auditor, then became a county commissioner. A lot of legislators in big counties took a local government path. In 1978, Rhodes got Voinovich to run for lieutenant governor with him—by then the governor and lieutenant governor ran as a team. After they won, Voinovich had about as much influence with Rhodes as Democrat Dick Celeste had when he was lieutenant governor along with Rhodes. Voinovich got tired of that quickly, and he left to become mayor of Cleveland. He was a successful mayor, serving for about ten years. He was out of Columbus again, so I didn't see much of him.

In 1988, Voinovich ran against Howard Metzenbaum for the U.S. Senate. It was an ill-fated campaign, where he made the terrible mistake of accusing Metzenbaum of being soft on child pornography. He got his butt handed to him. But I remember thinking when it came time for the next gubernatorial election, "Don't write him off on the basis of that one campaign because if he realized his mistake and can correct it, he can be a formidable candidate."

In 1990, Voinovich ran against Attorney General Anthony Celebrezze for governor. My feeling was that Voinovich was the odds-on favorite because people wanted a change after eight years of Celeste—and didn't want another guy where the first four letters of his last name were the same as Celeste's. Voinovich ran a good campaign and won. And he was reelected in 1994, partly because his Democratic opponent, state Senator Rob Burch, was a very weak candidate.

Once in office, Voinovich followed his own slogans, "work harder and smarter" and "do more with less," at a time when there had to be cutbacks in state government because of the economy. He wanted to have his hands on everything, a real micromanager. He got this program called "Q Step," which was evaluating state personnel. He wanted to get into the bowels of government. Overall, his policies were effective but moderate. In fact, a lot of conservatives said, "He's not a Republican—he's a Democrat." Voinovich was largely untainted by scandals involving his brother Paul and his former chief of staff, Paul Mifsud. He went on to serve two terms in the U.S. Senate.

Voinovich was a change from Rhodes and Celeste because most of the time he didn't give a lot of funny or exciting things to write about, except when he occasionally lost his temper. He was sort of gray—not that he wasn't competent—but he wasn't as colorful to cover as those other two were. So, we just went along and put up with bland government for eight years. For sixteen years, in fact, because his successor, Governor Bob Taft, was even less colorful.

I also knew Taft from his time in the legislature. Like Voinovich, he got elected to a local government position, Hamilton County Commissioner. And like Voinovich, Rhodes also got Taft to run as lieutenant governor in 1986, but he lost along with Rhodes that year. Except for the fact that he was part of the Taft political dynasty, I never thought much about his prospects of becoming governor.

In 1990, Taft was elected as Ohio secretary of state when Voinovich was elected governor, and he was reelected in 1994 along with Voinovich. That is when I got to know him. So, Taft was well positioned to run for governor when Voinovich was term-limited in 1998. Taft beat Attorney General Lee Fisher for governor that year—a sort of Cincinnati-Cleveland clash—and Taft was reelected in 2002, partly because his opponent, Cuyahoga County Commissioner Tim Hagan, was a weak candidate.

Taft had a background in finance, and we knew he was wise about budgets. He had a modest and moderate agenda. He was also a micromanager. Ironically, Taft got in trouble because he wasn't careful enough about reporting golf outings paid for by lobbyists. He was charged with misdemeanors and became the first sitting Ohio governor to be charged with a crime. This scandal paved the way for Democratic governor Ted Strickland in 2006, but I had retired by then and didn't cover him in office.

The best thing about Bob Taft was that when he got with reporters at press parties or at off-the-record events, he could be very funny. But it never showed publicly. It was almost like when he got out in public or had to do a press conference, he knew everybody was watching him. He stiffened up—tightened up into the old Taft mode where he was very intense. But in private, he could be relaxed and very funny.

The Best, the Worst, and the Most Fun
Joe Hallett

As a political reporter, I covered what may have been the best and worst gubernatorial campaigns in Ohio in the modern era.

But the 1986 Ohio gubernatorial campaign was the most fun to cover. It was a rematch between Dick Celeste, who was the incumbent, and former governor Jim Rhodes, who was trying one final comeback for a fifth four-year term. It was his last hurrah—in every sense of the word.

In those days, everybody had campaign buses and drove all over the states. All the reporters would be with the candidates for interviews. Rhodes never remembered my name, so he called me "Blade," because I was with the *Toledo Blade*. In fact, he didn't remember anybody's name. One time Rhodes stops a speech and says, "In the back of the room there is the statehouse press corps. Let me introduce them to you." Then he says, "She's the *Plain Dealer*, he's the *Dispatch*, and he's the *Blade*."

One campaign swing went up to Norwalk, and Rhodes stopped at a little grocery store and went grocery shopping. He bought bread, Dutch loaf, and cheese—he loved Dutch loaf (a cold-cut made from coarse-ground pork and beef) and assumed everyone else did—went back to the bus and started to make sandwiches. He hands one to everybody, including me, and says, "Eat it!" I said, "Well Governor, I'm not a big fan of Dutch loaf." He says, "Eat it!" So, I choked it down.

The same night we stopped in Brian, Ohio. Rhodes had an event there, and then we headed out for Lima at the end of the day because we had a breakfast there. Just four of us were in the back of the bus. Rhodes had kicked off his shoes and was done for the day. He invited us all back, and he said, "Let's just talk! It's all off the record." So, we agreed to that. It was the first time I learned that this politician was no country bumpkin, despite his public persona. He was a brilliant man. I can't remember all that he talked about, but he waxed on about everything: all the world's problems with a depth of perception and perspective that was never on display publicly.

At one point he was hammering on, and then suddenly, his eyes closed, his head dropped, and he was quiet for what seemed like five minutes, but it was probably a minute. We were thinking, "Did he just die?" About the time one of us was going to go over and shake him, his eyes popped open. He picked up midsentence where he had left off. Of course, he was seventy-seven years old.

It turned out to be a disastrous campaign for Rhodes and the Republicans because he railed on about Celeste being pro-homosexual during the final debate in Cincinnati. Bob Taft told me he was embarrassed by Rhodes's behavior; he was Rhodes's running mate and eventually was elected governor himself.

The next gubernatorial race I covered was in 1990, between George Voinovich, the former mayor of Cleveland, and Attorney General Anthony Celebrezze. The Voinovich effort was the best-run campaign I have ever seen. I don't think anybody really saw Voinovich coming in 1990 because of his awful campaign for the U.S. Senate in 1988, when he lost badly to Howard Metzenbaum.

The key event was a Saturday morning press conference where Celebrezze made the dramatic announcement that he had switched from being anti-abortion to pro-abortion. After the press conference, reporters surrounded the podium and peppered him with questions. Among them was what looked like a TV cameraman filming the discussion. It turned out to be Mike Dawson, the Voinovich campaign's deputy press secretary. Their campaign had the footage of Celebrezze's event.

Then we found out Celebrezze had previously stated that he thought abortion was murder. That made it all the worse for him because he had flipped on the issue. This perception was reinforced by an interview with Tony and his wife Louisa. The reporter was probing Tony about his decision to change on the issue, and then he turns to Louisa and asks, "What do you think?" She said, "I disagree with Tony, I'm anti-abortion," and stated all her reasons. At that point, the gubernatorial campaign was essentially over.

The worst gubernatorial campaign I ever saw was the Democrats against Voinovich when he ran for reelection in 1994. The Democrats couldn't find anybody to run against him because his approval ratings were very high. It looked like a suicide mission. They finally talked State Senator Rob Burch into running.

Burch kicked off his campaign off with a breakfast in Dover, Ohio, where he got a big crowd because that's his hometown. It was a nice event. Then we went out to leave, and I said, "Senator, where is the busing? By the way, where are all the other reporters?" There were none: it was just me.

Burch said, "Well, since it's just you, I'm going to drive." So, he hops in his car, with his girlfriend in the front seat next to him, and I get in the back seat. His next event is in Akron, and then he's got one in Cleveland. By the time he gets to Akron, he is well over an hour late. The crowd is angry. He is almost two hours behind by the time he reaches Cleveland. The crowd has dwindled. It was a disaster from the get-go. It remained that way to Election Day.

The Honeymooners
Jerry Austin

In 1990, Anthony Celebrezze was running for Ohio governor, and I convinced him to go to New York City for some training because he was not a very good or comfortable public speaker. After the first day of training, I had arranged for us to go to dinner at a Japanese restaurant and had purchased two tickets to the hottest show on Broadway, *The Phantom of the Opera*.

Tony had served in Japan when he was in the navy and loved Japanese food. He was delighted about the restaurant, but he said, "I'm not going to the Broadway show."

I said, "You don't understand, Tony, I bought these tickets with my own money, and they're very difficult to get."

He said, "No, no, no. I'm going to go back to the hotel and watch drag races on ESPN."

I thought he was kidding, but he was not. So, he went back to the hotel after dinner, and I went to the theatre. There were people in line looking for somebody who either wanted to sell tickets or somebody that didn't show up. I saw this young couple standing there.

I asked them, "You're seeking tickets for tonight's show?"

"Yes, do you have tickets?"

"Yes."

"How much are they?"

"Well, are you here on your honeymoon?"

"Yes."

I gave them the tickets and walked away.

He's on Your Side

Tom Diemer

One of the most fascinating people I covered in Ohio politics was Howard Metzenbaum. He was elected repeatedly, but most people didn't know he was Jewish, liberal, rich, or from Cleveland. Of course, Howard didn't stress his background on the campaign trail. But I think that the secret to his success was that he was a fighter.

He had an ornery, kitchen-table style, saying to voters, "You've got a voice here! I'm going to raise some hell, but I'm raising that hell for you."

I can't tell you how many people told me, "I don't know if I agree with him on all this stuff, but by God, he's not like other politicians! He's not there sitting on his hands. He's out there fighting for us."

I was having lunch one time with a friend, and we were talking about the way people viewed Metzenbaum. I said, "How did he manage that? How did this Jewish millionaire from Cleveland, who is to the left of ninety percent of his constituents, serve nineteen years in the U.S. Senate? What was his secret?"

My friend took a cocktail napkin, scribbled on it, and handed it to me.

It read: "He's on your side."

In his own way, Howard was like other skilled politicians such as Jack Kennedy or Ike Eisenhower: his appeal transcended Democrat/Republican and left/right labels. He was just there fighting for the little guy and fighting for Ohio.

Another thing is that he was an impeccable dresser. He looked crisp. He looked fresh. He looked ready to go.

Howard's fortune began in an interesting way—with airport parking. When he was in the state legislature in the 1940s, he used to fly from Cleveland to and from Columbus, probably the only legislator to do that in those days. He would look down as the plane landed and see cars just parked in a field, just spread around in an unpaved lot without marked spaces or anything. There he walked back to his car through weeds and mud. He wondered, "Why do we do it this way?"

So, he went to the airport people and said, "Look, why don't I set up the parking for you?"

They said, "What do you mean set up the parking?"

"You hire me; I'll be a concessionaire. We'll put a blacktop on the field, make little spaces for the cars, and we'll charge."

"Charge? Charge for parking? I don't know that we should charge for parking."

"We'll charge a nominal fee just to cover the cost, you'll see."

That is how Airport Parking of America was launched by Howard Metzenbaum and his partner, Ted Bonda. It seems so obvious now. But like a lot of good politicians, he understood mobility and transportation, and how important it was for people to be able to move around.

What This Car Can Do

Jerry Austin

In 1972, businessman Ted Bonda was taking some Democratic officeholders up to Cleveland to view some television spots.

Bonda was driving his red Rolls Royce. One of the passengers was a car afficionado and asked a lot of questions about the performance of the Rolls. He kept asking, "What can this car do?"

Finally, Bonda said, "Wait, I'll show you."

When he drove into Cleveland, he came to a major intersection that was closed for construction with a sign that said "No Left Turn" and a cop directing the heavy traffic.

Bonda pulls into the intersection, sticks his hand out of the window, and motions to the cop he wants to make a left turn.

The cop waves him through.

Bonda said, "That's what this car can do."

A Matter of Choice

Jerry Austin

One day in 1978, when I was running Anthony Celebrezze's campaign for secretary of state, I walked into the office, and Tony called me over.

He says, "Here, fill this out."

"What is this?" I asked.

He said, "It's a questionnaire on abortion."

"I'm not filling this out," I said and started to throw it in the garbage.

"Give it to me," Tony said.

He starts filling it out and writes that abortion is murder.

I'm thinking, obviously I'm not going to change his mind on this issue. We'll need to make the best of it—at least he may get some anti-abortion votes in that election.

Jump ahead twelve years to 1990: Tony is now Ohio attorney general and running for governor against Republican George Voinovich, the former Cleveland mayor. Both candidates were opposed to abortion.

Tony said to me: "Put together a group of women who may have a problem with me because of my position on abortion."

I said, "okay," and I called Cindy Lazarus.

Cindy got about a dozen women together. Just Tony and I were sitting in Cindy's living room, and each one was saying who she was and why she was there.

Then we got to Karen Schwarzwalder. Karen said, "Let's cut the bullshit—we're not supporting you."

"What do you mean? You supported me in the past despite this issue," Tony said.

Karen replied, "Yeah, well, you're wrong on the abortion issue."

I said, "Well, Voinovich is wrong on this issue, too."

She said: "Yeah, we're not supporting Voinovich either. We're sitting it out. So, no money, no volunteers, none of that."

Then I said, "Excuse me, may I see a show of hands of the women here who had to make a decision and at least contemplated abortion as an option?"

Eleven out the twelve there raised their hands.

"Okay, I apologize," I continued, "But how many of you chose to have an abortion?"

None of them raised their hands. Now, maybe they didn't want to admit it, but it was a stark difference.

Tony said, "What?"

"Tony, you don't understand," I said. "This is about a woman's right to choose. It's not about pro-abortion or anti-abortion. Nobody says, 'Let's go have a soda, see a movie, and have an abortion.'"

All of a sudden, a light goes on for Tony.

Later he told me, "I was brainwashed by the Catholic Church."

So now, I've got Tony educated—but perhaps overeducated: he wanted to switch sides and become pro-abortion.

I said, "Tony, I've spent that last year telling reporters that the worst thing a candidate can do is switch sides on an issue when the candidate has a history with an issue like abortion."

Tony said, "I don't care. I need to switch."

His wife, Louisa was going nuts. She was super Catholic and didn't want to hear about killing someone.

Not only did Tony switch positions on abortion, but he became a raving pro-abortion maniac.

I said to Tony, "I didn't take you into that room with women to change your lifelong position."

Tony said, "Well, after I heard their views, what did you want me to do, continue as a pro-life candidate?"

I said, "If you and Voinovich have the same position on abortion, then the issue doesn't matter to women who care about abortion. But you can recognize their concerns and talk about women's rights in other ways, so you can appeal to them on other issues."

In fact, Tony's newfound zeal didn't help him with many pro-choice women voters: they just thought that he changed his views for political reasons.

His campaign was over—as a matter of choice.

Social Change
Sandy Theis

Social change comes about in two ways—you either let it evolve, or you kick it in the ass. I decided to start kicking it in the ass, shifting from reporting on politics as a journalist to advocating for equality in sexual matters as a consultant. I've never seen a change this dramatic, not just for gays but for straight women and men too.

One factor was the nastiness of the politics. It just got so mean and so over the top. For example, Citizens for Community Values (CCV)—the group that did the Ohio gay marriage ban in 2004—was trying to pass legislation designed to cripple the adult entertainment industry. I was getting tired of right-wing phonies, advocates of "moral values" who were porn addicts, married and divorced multiple times. And they were so good at summing up their views with the word "freedom." But whose freedom? Nobody was pushing back on these questions.

I figured if CCV was for banning strip clubs, then I was against it. So, I got hired by the "dancers"—some people called them "strippers," but I called them "dancers." I got to know these women and got to like them. Most of them were single moms or they were going to college. I learned that their work paid well. One time we were discussing how much they earned, and I asked, "Tell me, on a good day how much to you make and how much on a bad day?" It turned out I was the least paid person at the table—and the only one working full time.

I helped these women tell their stories. When they testified before the legislative committee, I had them wear pink T-shirts that said "Dancers for Democracy." I got lots of "atta-girls" for doing it, but it wasn't great marketing: I just wanted the lawmakers to stop leering at the women, and instead, focus on their unconstitutional bill. I found that lots of people said, "Wait a minute. These are all adults. Why do we care? Why is this an issue?" In the end, the anti-dancer bill was so watered down that it was meaningless. I also learned that some legislators who supported the bill frequented local strip clubs, but the dancers had too much integrity to out them.

Generational change was another factor. My kids had an impact on changing my mind when the strip club issue was in the news. We were talking about it at the dinner table. My son had a friend who posed naked for *Playboy,* and she got $50,000 for the photo shoot. Then her dad said, "I'll pay you $50,000 not to do it." But she did it anyway, and it launched her career with some TV show. I said, "Are you kidding? Why would a woman demean herself like that?" I got blowback from my kids. They don't see anything wrong with it. I was stunned.

When our son was about fifteen, there was a kid from his class who was sent home from a public school for wearing a T-shirt that said, "I support gay marriage." So, he came home and talked to his lawyer father about why that was unconstitutional—and launched protests throughout the entire week in the school where kids came in wearing those T-shirts. I came home, and there were fifteen hand-painted T-shirts hanging from my light fixtures.

One of the TV networks called, and they wanted to put our son on TV. I said, "Okay, but people are going to think you're gay." I wasn't telling him that I didn't think he should do it; I just wanted him to know what some of the consequences would be.

He said," Yeah, I'm tall, I'm blonde, a snappy dresser. Mom, I don't care. Being gay, it's like being left-handed. It can be inconvenient sometimes, but it's no big deal."

A local gay-rights magazine asked the kids to write an article about the issue. Some parents called me and asked, "Have you seen that publication?" I said, "Look at the sports section in the newspaper. You'll see ads for titty bars and that kind of stuff. What's the difference?"

I was worried that the article would not be grammatically correct, so I wanted to see it first. They let me read it before publication. It was perfect! I sat there and cried in my family room. After it was published, some other parents called and said, "The kids were wonderful. We feel really embarrassed that we voted for the gay marriage ban."

The public school eventually retracted their unconstitutional T-shirt policy and issued a statement that said, "Some days we teach the kids, and some days they teach us." I thought was a classy thing to do.

A Really Odd Moment
Mike Curtin

During Jim Rhodes's final gubernatorial campaign in 1986, I sometimes wondered whether the Rhodes campaign had someone check up on me because of a story I was writing.

I was investigating a group called Ohioans for Decency and Health. It appeared to be a shell group created by the Rhodes people and Rhodes allies to tarnish his opponent, Governor Richard Celeste. The group took out full-page ads in newspapers across the state, including my own paper, the *Columbus Dispatch*, portraying Celeste as too friendly to the gay community. The ads claimed that if Celeste were reelected, such views would lead to all sorts of bad outcomes for the state of Ohio.

I had a couple of good sources who led me to believe I could connect Ohioans for Decency and Health to the Rhodes campaign. This link was important because Rhodes and his people were on record as saying they had nothing to do with the group. But at the same time, Rhodes brought up the allegation in debates with Celeste. Eventually, I was able to break the story, showing the link between the Rhodes campaign and this anti-gay front group.

While I was working on the story, I was getting some strange phone calls. A couple of callers seemed to be soliciting me, wondering whether I was interested in some sort of gay relationship.

It made me wonder, does somebody in the Rhodes campaign, possibly Jim Rhodes himself, think that the motivation for my investigation into Ohioans for Decency and Health was because I was gay myself? Did they think I was in the closet, and maybe they could threaten to expose me, and put an end to my investigation? Did political operatives have such convoluted logic?

It was a really odd moment.

The Conversation

Dan Mowbray

As the owner of The Media Group, Inc., a television-radio production company specializing in Democratic candidates, I was deeply involved in the two successful campaigns for Dick Celeste for governor of Ohio (1982 and 1986). It was no secret to our competition in 1986, the election team of our opponent former governor James A. Rhodes, that I knew the strategy of the campaign as well as what TV commercials were going on the air next.

Our home was in German Village—the Columbus, Ohio, equivalent of Georgetown—and was only ten convenient minutes from our office. To get away from the election madness and let our beloved golden retriever, Marlowe, outdoors, I would often dash home for lunch. My wife, Alta, and I had a home answering machine with a microcassette player. One lunch hour during that time, I walked into the kitchen to see the red light flashing. Nothing strange about that.

But what I heard next astounded me.

It was a conversation between Jim Ruvolo, chairman of the Ohio Democratic Party and some lady I had never heard of. And let me emphasize here. *It was not a message for ME*. It was a conversation between them. In fact, I'd never called Jim from my home, nor conversely had he called me at home—ever. With my imagination going wild, I quickly suspected one thing: wiretapping that had gone awry. I felt like I was Harry Caul, the Gene Hackman character in the movie *The Conversation* who overhead something he shouldn't have, leading to all sorts of bad things.

I immediately took the cassette and a handheld player downtown to the Ohio Democratic Headquarters, where I met with Jim. While doing the usual greetings in his office, I used hand motions to guide him into the hallway where we wouldn't be overheard. "What's this all about?" he asked, obviously perplexed at my strange behavior.

"Just listen," I replied mysteriously, and played the recording.

"How in the hell did you get that?" he asked after it was finished.

"First, did you call me at home?" I asked.

"No," he said.

Then I told him how I had found the recording and gave him the tape.

"Just be careful what you say in the office until you get this sorted out," I cautioned him, in my best Harry Caul impersonation.

Then a disappointment of a sorts: Jim had the headquarters swept from stem to stern and the technicians found nothing. But I ask you: How did Jim's conversation with that woman end up on my answering machine? There is still *no* legitimate answer.

Do I still think my phone or Jim's was tapped? You betcha!

But don't take my word that strange things can happen over the telephone. Just ask Harry Caul . . .

The Human Touch
Bob Ney

Toward the end of 1993, the former Ohio Senate colleagues who were then in Congress—Dave Hobson, John Kasich, and Paul Gillmor—came into my office and said, "You've got to run for Congress next year."

They were excited, saying "Newt Gingrich is going to be the next Speaker of the House of Representatives because we're going to take control of the Congress."

I said, "Well, I talked to friends of mine, including Neil Clarke and Curt Steiner, and they say, 'It's not going to happen.'"

"Look, I'm chairman of the finance committee in the Ohio Senate," I went on, "I'm going to be president of the Senate because all chairmen of the Senate finance committee become presidents of the Senate. I want to run for governor. That's all I ever wanted to do is run for governor of Ohio. I didn't want to run for Congress."

Anyways, these guys just kept coming in. They talked about the prestige of being in Congress, the nice salary and terrific pension, and the opportunity to travel.

I'm like, "No, I'm not running. No, no, no. I can't even stand Congress. I give speeches as state senator against Congress."

So, a couple of things happened.

First, I was at a graduation party and Bob Bennett, the chairman of the Ohio Republican Party, was there. Bennett said, "You got to run for Congress. You can take out Doug Applegate (the congressman who followed Wayne Hays). You know, Wayne was dynamic, but Doug was just a nice guy."

But I said, "Bob, I don't want to run for Congress."

Second, they commissioned a poll. Neil Clarke and Curt Steiner call me over to my office, and they've got this poll sitting there. They say, "You can beat Doug Applegate. You can beat him; this is in the poll."

I said, "Guys, I love beating incumbents, I beat Wayne Hays, nobody was tougher. I think I could beat Applegate, but I don't want to run for Congress."

Third, I got a phone call from Bob Bennett. He goes, "You need to do me a favor. You need to go out and see Newt Gingrich. He wants to see you. Just spend ten minutes and tell the man you don't want to run. I promised you'd go out to see him."

"Well, un-promise it," I said. "Because I'm not going to waste a guy's time. I've never met Newt Gingrich. I'm not going to run out there just to tell him 'No.'"

Bob said, "Please just do me a favor, that's all I'm asking you. Just go out, we'll pay for everything, fly you out, just go out."

I finally said, "Okay."

Actually, I had a very distant connection with Gingrich. Earlier, Dave Hobson had called asking for some help. Newt's wife Marianne was from Salem, Ohio, in Columbiana County. Her brother, Ray, could not get a highway job—he had three kids, and he was a nice guy. So, I called the highway department and said, "What in the hell is wrong with this guy? You penalize him because he's Newt Gingrich's brother-in-law?" Well, they hired him up in Columbiana County. I never told anyone about it—it was just a favor for a colleague.

So, I fly out to Washington, D.C., to see Newt Gingrich, and I take my chief of staff, Dave DiStefano, with me. We arrive at the Capitol, Room 209, right off the floor of the House of Representatives.

Before I opened the door, I said to Dave, "Here's the game plan: We'll go in; I'll tell Newt no, and then we'll just go drinking."

He said, "Okay, but you're not running?"

"I'm not running, Dave, you know that. I told everybody I'm not running."

I opened the door, and it was a small room full of people, with maybe nine or ten people doing different things. I said to the woman that was standing there, "Wow, I'm so sorry. Where's the secretary?" She said, "Are you Senator Ney? I'm sorry, but can you step out in the hall?"

I was thinking, how rinky-dink! I had a nicer office in the state capitol that opened to the floor of the Senate finance committee. I mean, it was fantastic, and I was in a good position to go on and do great things.

So, we got called in and sat down. There was Newt, sitting in a chair right in front of me.

Newt said, "Before we start, I want to personally thank you for what you did for my brother-in-law."

I said, "Sure, no problem. I'm shocked Dave Hobson told you I did it. Why didn't he take credit?"

Newt laughed. Then he started talking. He didn't talk about the prestige of Congress or the benefits of being in Congress—salary, pensions, travel. He talked for forty-five minutes about the future of the country and his idea for a "Contract with America."

He was mesmerizing.

He looked at me and said, "There is a seat in Ohio we can't win. There hasn't been a Republican in it for over fifty-five years, but just one time, and before that it was forty years Democratic. It has a sixteen-percent Republican index. We can't win it, but you can."

"The question is," he went on, "I need nineteen more people in these critical seats to change the course of this county. If you say 'yes,' you can be one of those. I've got to get eighteen more people to save this county. If you say 'no,' I've got to find the nineteenth. I need you to do what's right for America, your grandchildren, and your great-grandchildren."

I said, "I'll run."

"Thanks, I'll come and campaign for you."

"No offense, but just stay out of my district. I don't know you, but they don't like you there. I have a union district. You've got to stay out of my district."

And that's how it happened—the human touch.

Anyway, I walked outside with Dave DiStefano. He looked at me and said, "What the hell did you just do?"

"I changed my mind."

"What the hell we going to do now?"

"Get drunk, and then we're going to run for Congress."

It turned out that Doug Applegate decided to retire, leaving an open seat. It was a tough campaign, but a lot easier than running against Wayne Hays for state representative back in 1980.

I won Wayne Hays's old seat, and three other Ohio guys beat incumbent Democrats: Frank Cremeans in Appalachia, Steve LaTourette near Cleveland, and Steve Chabot near Cincinnati. These four seats were critical to the Republicans taking control of Congress for the first time in forty years.

Right away, I wanted to be on the House Administration Committee. John Boehner, an Ohio colleague, was on it, and he wanted the committee disbanded.

Newt Gingrich put me on the House Administration Committee. He said, "You'd be good for it. You're a seasoned legislator; you know how things operate. House Administration would be good for you."

Thirty days in Newt Gingrich called me and said, "How would you like to be the vice chairman of the House Administration today?"

I said, "Isn't somebody else in line?"

"That's not what I asked you," he said, "Do you want to be the first vice chairman of a full committee in this new class of all Republicans? You want to be the first committee chairman out of your class eventually?"

"Yeah."

"I'm going to make you first vice chairman today. I'll take care of the other member with something else."

I was the first chairman out of that "Contract with America" class of members, then I got my chairmanship of the House Administration Committee under Speaker Dennis Hastert in 1999.

Soon we had an "Ohio Mafia" in the House of Representatives: John Boehner and Deb Price were in leadership; Dave Hobson and Ralph Regula were "Cardinals" on the Appropriations Committee; I was chairman of House Administration Committee; John Kasich was on the House Budget committee; Paul Gillmor on Energy and Commerce; Steve LaTourette was on Transportation; and Steve Chabot on Small Business.

Ohioans seemed to be everywhere.

Parking Permits
Nick Zimmers

We had a place out in Colorado where we would go on vacation, and we got to know a guy who was the president of the local homeowner's association.

We were having dinner, and the guy says, "Do you know a lawyer or anybody who can help us? We need a post office. We have asked the U.S. Postal Service and were denied. There are several thousand people in this community, and people have to drive to another town eight miles away just to pick up the mail at the general post office."

I said, "Before you do anything, let me make a phone call."

So, I called a friend, Ohio congressman Bob Ney, who was the chairman of the House Administration Committee.

I said, "We have a situation here in Colorado."

Bob said, "Colorado?"

I said, "Yeah, could you help us get a post office for our community? Maybe write a letter to the local congressman for us or something?"

Bob said, "Let me see what I can do."

The next time we were in Colorado, the homeowner's association guy told me, "Well, we got our post office."

Later I asked Bob, "How did you do that?

Bob said, "I control the parking permits on Capitol Hill."

Off the Clock

Bob Ney

So, one day I'm on an airplane flying back to Ohio from Washington, D.C., with my colleagues, Congressmen Paul Gillmor and John Kasich.

This older veteran gets on the plane. He's got his purple and gold legion hat on and other regalia. He recognized us, and he said, "Oh, Congressmen Gillmor, Ney, and Kasich!"

John, he's got his newspaper, looks up and goes, "I'm off the clock."

Another time, Congressman Steve LaTourette and I go up to an Ohio State football game in Columbus.

So, we're sitting there, and we look down and we see John and his girlfriend (who later became his wife) coming up through the stands, about fifteen rows down from us.

Steve starts yelling, "Kasich!" I start yelling, "Kasich!"

John doesn't look up at us, but he puts his hand up in the air like swatting us away.

We get back to Congress on Tuesday. John comes on the floor of the House and says, "Guys, I'm so sorry. Somebody said that it was you guys yelling at me. I thought it was constituents."

Unbelievable Energy

Terry Casey

An important thing to know about Governor John Kasich was his unbelievable energy.

That's why in 1978, Kasich—unemployed at the time, not even from Ohio, with an ethnic-sounding name in a district where ethnic names were unheard of—beat state senator Robert O'Shaughnessy, the heir to a political dynasty, and became one of the youngest state senators ever.

Many politicians tell you they're campaigning hard or tell you they're going door-to-door, but Kasich was actually doing it. Day after day after day, he had a relentless drive and energy. He was so persistent that people backed him just to stop his pestering.

In 1982, Kasich beat Congressman Bob Shamansky—the only Republican to defeat an incumbent Democrat in a very tough year for the GOP. He then served eighteen years in the House of Representatives, rising to become the chairman of the House Budget committee. He brought that kind of energy to Congress and developed something of a maverick image with unique views on issues.

Kasich was a policy wonk. He really liked to focus on the bowels of government. I saw this side of him when he ran for Ohio governor in 2010, and I played his opponent, Governor Ted Strickland, in the debate preparation. I had a good bit of fun going after Kasich on details—he was tough to out-detail. You saw the same style in Kasich's two terms as Ohio governor. "Irritated" is a word you would hear about Kasich: some people got frustrated with his drive, and he got impatient with some people's lack of focus.

These things were problematic when Kasich was running for the Republican presidential nomination in 2016. He kept wanting to talk about the detailed substance of major issues, but the news media was more obsessed with what I call "Kardashian" style journalism—you know, Trump, and unless you attacked Trump, you got ignored. The news media's coverage of policy substance had gotten so shallow.

Kasich had a strategy to do well in the New Hampshire primary. He worked his ass off there, and that put him second to Trump. But he only had a week in South Carolina after New Hampshire, and he couldn't achieve the same kind of results. He also had difficulty raising money, so he couldn't compete effectively in the remaining states. Kasich became sort of a "kinder, gentler" alternative to Trump—which made people in Ohio laugh. But because of his energy, Kasich was the last to leave the race to Trump.

Godspeed, Issue 2
John Polidori

The Tea Party tornado struck in 2011, fueled by vast amounts of right-wing money. It resulted in the loss of Democratic congressional majorities and blunted the great wave of hope engendered by Barack Obama's election two years earlier.

At the state level, hegemonic Republican "trifectas" littered the landscape, Ohio being one of them—places where they controlled all of state government.

For organized labor, it served as one hell of a wake-up call. The Koch Brothers' political organization, Americans for Prosperity, moved immediately to attack organized labor through the passage of so-called right-to-work laws that would weaken both private and public sector unions.

Going a step further, the Koch forces focused like a laser on gutting labor's public sector collective bargaining rights. Fewer members meant reduced political influence in terms of volunteers and funds, while weakening the voice of unions that served as a countervailing societal force.

Wisconsin possessed the oldest public sector collective bargaining law in the country and served as the first major point of attack. Other states with labor presence—Michigan, Ohio, Missouri, Indiana, and even Maine, Florida, and New Hampshire also got hit. But the real goal was to destroy the Democratic Party's great blue Midwest wall, cornerstoned for decades by organized labor.

Wisconsin's new governor, Scott Walker, was the Koch poster boy for public sector union destruction. In Michigan, the attack targeted private sector unions (think UAW), since public sector unions had been previously weakened.

In Ohio, the new governor, Republican John Kasich (a former U.S. congressman), had just defeated Democratic incumbent Ted Strickland (also a former U.S. congressman). Kasich moved in lockstep with Walker, seeking to take advantage of the new Republican legislative majority in both chambers.

The vehicle, Senate Bill 5, served like the attack in Wisconsin, was aimed directly at public sector collective bargaining rights. But Kasich and allies made the mistake of including the bargaining rights of local police. For weeks state capitol demonstrations and occupation importantly raised public awareness, yet the Republican trifecta exerted relatively swift legislative action, passing SB5 in just a couple of months.

The National Education Association had assigned me to the national AFL-CIO headquarters in D.C., where we worked to assist the state-level union defense campaigns and advise the council of national union presidents on funding priorities.

Our national campaign manager, Aaron Pickrell, knew Ohio well. He had run Obama's 2008 presidential campaign and served as senior adviser to the 2010 Strickland reelection campaign. We understood that Ohio offered a tactical backstop not available in many other states—the citizen initiative to recall enacted legislation.

Once Senate Bill 5 was enacted, "We Are Ohio" was birthed. With only 231,000 valid signatures needed for statutory recall, the historically unprecedented labor-organized coalition met complicated county requirements by submitting over 1.3 million signatures to start the recall rolling (the previous Ohio record had been 813,000 signatures). Over 70 percent of these signatures—largely collected by trained volunteers—were validated.

With a special November election in 2011 (an off-year election), we faced a steep recall mountain. Over the next six months, labor union members walked neighborhoods, taking advantage of summer weather to knock on doors and put a face on the voices of people sentenced to silence.

Our pollster, Lisa Grove, and media consultant, Will Robinson, distilled how Ohioans had understood the previous winter's shenanigans in Columbus. Our campaign message centered on the value-based idea that the voices of "everyday heroes"—firefighters, nurses, teachers, and police—should not suffer silencing because they are the people who have "had the backs of Ohioans."

As our television, radio, and online advertising took hold, I remember to this day arriving at voters' doors, starting my doorstep quick pitch, only to be interrupted:

"Oh, you're with the firemen, teachers, nurses, and cops, right?"

"Yep, I am."

"Don't worry. This is nuts. We're with you."

Never talking about labor or contractual rights, it was simply about "Protecting Our Everyday Heroes" whose public service was valued and appreciated by Ohioans. No ideology. No partisanship. Ohioans came to understand that what had happened was just plain mean.

Our trained debaters carried the message on the evening news, at local events, and in major debates and presentations across the state. But as we began to prepare for the closing argument, our campaign manager, A. J. Stokes, was reaching for a fresh idea in the final, closing advertisement.

When discussing the content of our last opinion survey, I suggested that we test the name recognition and favorability of the first American to orbit the Earth, former U.S. senator John Glenn. A few folks in the room—colleagues and longtime Ohio operatives—laughed and had fun pooh-poohing it: "Isn't he retired?" "He's too old." "No one remembers him."

But Lisa, our pollster, said: "I like it. Let's include his name." Not a big deal, right?

When the results came back a week later, the Glenn numbers, like many of his aeronautical missions, were stratospheric—over 70 percent favorability among all voters among Republicans, Democrats, and Independents alike.

Next job: convince Senator Glenn to star in the campaign's closing commercial. One of our two lead debaters, Dale Butland, had been Senator Glenn's former press secretary and chief of staff. He agreed to make the ask. Glenn agreed, provided he could write his own commercial. He eventually considered a commercial written by Will, our media consultant. The final script wound up being a combination of the two.

The closing line, however, was Glenn-authored language: "Here in Ohio, we don't turn our backs on those who watch ours."

We'd hoped for a resounding win, but the final numbers shocked all of us: a complete repudiation—62 to 35 percent—with victory in eighty-three of Ohio's eighty-eight counties.

A few days later, I was sipping coffee with the opposition campaign manager, whom I had gotten to know, and he asked: "How the heck did you come up with the idea to get America's greatest contemporary hero to cut your last ad?"

Dedicated Staffer
Mark Weaver

I was the general and media consultant for Betty Montgomery in her races for the Ohio state senate, attorney general, and state auditor. In 2006, she was running for another term as attorney general. Her opponent was State Senator Marc Dann, a criminal defense lawyer from Youngstown.

Our opposition research discovered that Dann once represented a child molester in court. As part of his argument for leniency for the child molester, Dann told the judge "Your honor, my client was just trying to reach out to the children in the neighborhood."

Of course, that's a ridiculous thing to say when you're defending a child molester. We polled it, and voters thought the insensitivity of such a statement disqualified a candidate for the office of attorney general.

I decided to get a TV spot ready. We needed a photo of the child molester, but no picture was publicly available. We did some research and got an address of a trailer park in the Youngstown area. I asked a junior-level staffer (who wasn't paid very much) to find a picture of the criminal. I said, "Don't come back till you have a picture of the child molester."

So, the staffer sits outside the house for hours and realizes this guy isn't coming out. The child molester had figured out that we were trying to get his picture. The staffer goes back to his hotel and then comes back the next day to sit outside for a couple hours. And then the child molester calls the police. The police come and they ask the staffer what he's doing. He tells them some far-fetched story, and they leave him alone.

Then finally the staffer thinks that the way to get the child molester to open the door is to send him flowers. He pays a flower delivery service to get the flowers delivered and waits as the child molester comes out to receive the flowers from the delivery person. The staffer was deeply disappointed because only he got a photo of the molester reaching one arm out the cracked door to grab the flowers. The staffer came back with nothing. He's now a seasoned political professional.

However, this effort is a testament to what a campaign staffer who's dedicated to the cause and has a little bit of creativity would do to advance the needs of a campaign.

BOB

Jerry Austin

In 2004, I helped create "Bring Ohio Back" (BOB). We raised money to bring celebrities into Ohio to Get Out the Vote (GOTV) for John Kerry. Among the celebrities were Susan Sarandon, Paul Newman, Kevin Bacon, Kyra Sedgwick, Marisa Tomei, Joe Pantoliano, Steve Buscemi, Fisher Stevens, Kathy Najimy, Chad Lowe, Matt Dillon, and Timothy Hutton.

I was dispatched to Los Angeles to represent BOB at a fundraiser at the famous Viper Room featuring Elvis Costello. The next morning, flying back to Cleveland and upgraded, I found myself seated next to Martin Sheen. He was reading his Bible. I interrupted to say hello, and I realized he was one of our guest celebrities for the coming weekend. We had a terrific conversation about politics, *The West Wing*, and the fact he was born and raised in Ohio.

Upon landing, I told him I was headed to Cleveland's private airport where I was to pick up the other celebrity for the weekend—Robert Redford. He had never met Redford. I replied, "You will in a few hours."

Redford had agreed to come to Cleveland because of my friend Joyce Deep, who was his political adviser. I had asked Joyce to bring him to Ohio several times, but it never happened. I asked again and, as luck would have it, he was done with a speaking engagement in Rochester and could fly to Cleveland for most of the weekend.

I had never met Redford. As I waited for the private jet to land, I started rehearsing my first words to him. The plane landed, and Joyce and Redford started walking toward me. Before I could say anything, Redford exclaimed "Where's the bathroom?" My first words to him, pointing to the terminal, were "First door on the right."

Redford and Sheen met at the hotel and became fast friends. We held a successful fundraiser featuring the two stars.

At the end of the weekend, I had two responsibilities. One, making sure transportation was provided for Sheen to the airport—after he attended church. And two, driving Joyce and Redford to the airport. I went to the hotel to say goodbye to Sheen. He took a bundle of papers out of his bag, wrote something on it, and gave it to me. I was in a hurry and said, "Thanks, hope to see you again."

While driving Redford to the airport to catch a scheduled flight to Los Angeles, Joyce said, "Bob, ask Jerry the question." He was slumped down in the back seat, sat up, and asked, "You remember *The Candidate*?"

"Of course," I responded.

He continued, "I have been working on a sequel for almost thirty years. Here's where I am with the story. My character eventually becomes vice president. The president dies. I become president. My question, do I revert to my very liberal past, or do I continue to sell out?"

I responded, "Is this picture fact or fiction?'

He laughed. A sequel has never been made.

And the bunch of papers given to me by Martin Sheen? An autographed copy of the original script for *The West Wing* pilot.

II. Campaigns

Robert Redford and Philadelphia Hookers
Mark Siegel

In 1982, I spent considerable time raising money for Democratic candidates for the United States Senate. One of the races I was particularly interested in was the young Democratic mayor of Salt Lake City Ted Wilson's challenge to Utah conservative Republican Orrin Hatch.

Mark Brand worked for me at the time, and he had a working relationship with the Sundance Institute headed by Robert Redford. Redford was an environmental activist and was a strong supporter of Mayor Wilson. I was asked by the Wilson campaign to put together a Jewish-oriented fundraiser for Wilson in Philadelphia and was promised that Robert Redford had agreed to attend, which was certain to expand the potential money that could be raised.

I called one of the members of my political action committee, Sonny Dogol, and he arranged for a friend of his with a large central Philadelphia apartment to host the event. Redford and I were staying at the Rittenhouse Hotel. I had a room adjoining Redford's suite.

The cocktail event went very well and raised a great deal of money. Redford was personable and agreed to pictures with each of the attendees. He also delivered a rousing speech. After the fundraiser, Redford and I went out for a late dinner. I made a reservation in the city's best French restaurant under my name, attempting to preserve Redford's anonymity. Although people stared and pointed during dinner, it was quiet and friendly; we talked politics. What we didn't know is that the word had gone out from patrons of the restaurant and people who had seen us enter that Robert Redford was in the restaurant. By the time we left, there must have been five hundred people congregated outside hoping to get a look at the movie star.

We returned to the hotel and said goodnight. Thirty minutes later there was a knock on my door. I opened it up to see two very attractive, if a bit overdressed and heavily made-up women, just standing there. One of these women said to me that our fundraiser host had sent them for Mr. Redford and me. It took me awhile to understand what they were saying. I was flustered, probably bright red, and stuttered that this was very nice of him, but we wouldn't be needing their services.

One of the women said, "But we're already paid for."

I said, "Well, that's great for you, you have your money, and you don't have to work."

I started to close the door, but one of the women was arguing with me, telling me to check with Mr. Redford.

Then I realized she was the prostitute that was planning to sleep with Robert Redford. The one that was assigned to me had already run halfway down the hall to the elevator.

I told Redford at breakfast what had happened. He said I had done the right thing.

It was funny, but also sad.

My thought was how the image of Washington, D.C., and politics was shaped by images of corruption, sex, and money. The events of the previous night were something out of the novel *Advise and Consent*. That wasn't the Washington, D.C. I knew, but years later hearing about the pervasive sexual harassment on Capitol Hill, maybe it was a bit more accurate of a portrayal than I had realized.

Politics of Ill Repute

Katherine Rogers

In 1986, I was a campaign manager for Governor John Evans of Idaho, who was running for the United States Senate against incumbent Republican Steve Symms.

The second stop on our announcement tour was Wallace County. It was a Democratic area, but it was different than any other place in the state. Because of the silver mines, there was gambling, prostitution, and drinking—it was illegal, but accepted.

The Republican attorney general had just closed the brothels in Wallace County. That caused a great amount of anger from the Democrats who owned the establishments and the casinos. They called me as campaign manager and said that unless the governor reopened the brothels, they wouldn't come to the event—and they would make sure no one came to the event.

I was faced with having no one at the second stop on the announcement tour and that would embarrass the governor. So, I went and asked him if he would reopen the brothels.

The governor said, "There's no way I can open them back up! They're illegal in the first place, and I can't as a governor turn back a decision of the attorney general. Besides one-third of the state is Mormon and would frown upon such a decision."

We were sitting in a hotel room trying to figure out what to do. What a pair: the governor, a straitlaced, non-drinking Mormon, and me, a nice girl from New Hampshire who didn't know a thing about prostitution.

I said, "What are we going to do? We can't go to the event in this county, and nobody would turn out. It's the most Democratic county in the state. How do you explain why nobody showed up? Because the state closed the brothels?"

The governor told me to fix it, and I didn't know what to do.

I decided to talk with the Democratic chair of the Wallace County party. He advised me to not do anything until the next day. He knew that the Republicans who owned shares in the brothels were angry too. The Republican attorney general rescinded his order. Our event took place as planned, although with a smaller turnout than anticipated.

Ironically, it was the Republicans that kept the houses of ill repute open.

Chippendale
John Zogby

In 2006, a young man in western Florida contacted me directly about polling a potential race challenging an undistinguished member of Congress.

Before the conference call, the young man sent me his bio and other vital information. I was bowled over: Ivy League undergraduate and law degrees, rising prominence with a local law firm, and a strong record of community and nonprofit activism. He was strikingly handsome, had a beautiful wife and a baby on the way.

So, what could possibly be a problem here?

"I was a Chippendale when I was in college," he told me.

"Does that mean you worked at Disney?" I wondered.

No, he had been a male stripper.

That's what could go wrong with this picture.

When we polled the district, voters loved everything about the guy—except for the male stripper history. Interestingly, it bothered men a whole lot more than it did women.

It was a game changer.

After he saw the results, my advice to him was simple: "Take a few years off and then run for president."

In Love with the Same Man
Phil Noble

South Carolina U.S. senator Fritz Hollings's second wife was called "Peatsy"—nobody knew her real name. Peatsy was an outspoken Southern belle who liked to give as good as she got. No shrinking violet, she was funny and totally unpredictable.

In 1984, Hollings and Peatsy were up in New Hampshire, where he was campaigning for the Democratic presidential nomination. The campaign wasn't going very well.

Very early one morning, the telephone rang in their cheap motel room and Peatsy answered the phone. It was a reporter asking if he could speak to Senator Hollings.

Peatsy held out the phone and said, "Hey there fella! Wake up! Wake up! Is your name Hollings, honey?"

Senator Hollings was not known for an overabundance of humility, and when Peatsy was once asked why she thought their marriage lasted so long, Peatsy said, "It's because Fritz and I are in love with the same man."

Iowa Campaign Cameos
Bob Leonard

I worked as a radio reporter in the small town of Pella, Iowa, for many years. I have lots of memories of meeting presidential candidates.

On the Fourth of July 2007, Barack Obama came to a house in Des Moines. It was a pretty hot day. Obama was starting his rise in the polls, and he was really moving. The media was out in back of the house, and everybody was there: the *New York Times*, the *Chicago Tribune*, *CNN*, and *Fox News*. Obama was talking to all these reporters. I'm the only press person looking away from Obama. I'm more interested in the media than the candidate.

Just before Obama was to speak somebody tapped me on the shoulder, "Would you like to speak with Mr. Obama afterwards?" And I said, "Absolutely." He said, "Meet me on the back porch."

My father-in-law was Barack Obama's father's roommate in college at the University of Hawaii. My father-in-law, who is a Republican, held baby Barack in his arms when they came home from the hospital. My father-in-law didn't like Obama's father at all, but he liked his mother.

While shaking Obama's hand I said, "My father-in-law was your father's roommate in college." He gave a double take and said, "What?" I repeated it, and he asked, "Do you have your father-in-law's phone number?" I said, "Yeah." I gave the number to a staffer. I'm thinking about all the controversy over Obama's birth certificate and if he was an American citizen.

After the interview, I turned to one of his aides and said, "There's all the media in the world there. Barack Obama could've spoken to anybody, but he picked me." The guy said, "Today in Iowa, there's no more important media than you." (By the way, Obama never called my father-in-law.)

In contrast, Hillary Clinton wouldn't have anything to do with me. Politicians are afraid they'll come out to Iowa and get cow poop on their shoes or something. Her campaign staff was not helpful. It is an untold story of how staffs can just blow it with voters.

I'm sitting in the barber's chair on Saturday at eight a.m. and other guys are sitting in the other chairs. A Clinton staffer comes in—the smartest lady you could imagine, very personable with lots of policy engagement.

She knew I was media, and so she asks the room, "You're going to caucus for Hillary?" Many of the guys who were there said, "No." Then she said, "Why not?" A guy would try to say why not, but of course, she knew more about policy, and she made the guy look like a fool in front of his buddies. She went around all the guys in the chairs, and they were all totally eviscerated by her logic and command of facts. She lost everybody in there.

Later, one guy said, "I have a boss like her, and I'm not going to caucus for Hillary."

John McCain's campaign was similar. I called to set up an interview with McCain when he came through Iowa. His people laughed at me and said, "We don't do small-market radio." Then they hung up. You know how that worked out for McCain.

Mitt Romney was always good in terms of interviews. One time we were over at Vermeer, Iowa, with a big media gaggle. We went outside for the TV people. Because I was local, I was brought down close to Romney. He looked out at the field across the road and asked, "What are those?" I said, "Those are soybeans." Romney said, "Oh, that's what they look like." It was pretty funny. You know, it would be a legitimate question on the east or west coasts, but in Iowa it was like asking what a banana looks like.

The former governor of Wisconsin Tommy Thompson also came through in 2007. I got on his bus. He just milked me during the interview with questions about Pella, Iowa, which was the next stop. Just kept asking me questions, "What are the schools? What's this? What's that?" I gave him a lecture on the history of the people in Pella. He used it all when we got to Pella. It was an incredible speech.

Speaking of people signaling things, after our interview was over, Thompson went back to the private part of the bus. I could just barely hear him. His shirt had fallen on the floor. Instead of picking it up, he called found a campaign assistant and scolded him in a whisper, "The shirt was on the floor. Go pick up my shirt." Well, it said a lot about him. An assistant was publicly chastised—the aides could see it, I could see it, but Tommy Thompson couldn't see it.

Donald Trump came to Des Moines in 2015. He flew in before he declared his candidacy. He invited a bunch of reporters on his plane. I went up with a gaggle of media people, maybe a dozen. Hope Hicks greeted us. She was delightful. I was introduced to Trump. He was a little taller than I thought he would be, with a gracious handshake. We were brought to the front of the plane. He described the plane—he was very proud of the rare woods and platinum. He was bragging, but he was very fussy because there were fifteen of us on his plane with cameras, microphones, and stuff. He didn't want us to soil or dent anything. Somebody had a boom mike, and he said, "You're going to hit the ceiling. Don't hit the ceiling." It felt like I was on Martha Stewart's plane. Some of the media asked good questions. Most of them asked why he rejected Shawn Johnson, the Olympic gold-medal gymnast on *The Apprentice*. It was very bizarre.

I took Trump's run seriously because two local conservative businessmen I respected took him seriously. I don't think the rest of the Des Moines media took him seriously.

In 2016, I had an interview set up with Bernie Sanders. I traveled to Des Moines to meet him. I got a call that said, "Something's come up. We're not going to have time for you." Twenty minutes later, I see a tweet about Bernie Sanders having breakfast and coffee with *The Washington Post* in Des Moines.

On the Record All the Time
David Yepsen

Many of the reporters I knew were sports reporters who switched over to politics. They loved the action of politics. Many of those reporters have basically retired. It is a totally different experience from forty years ago.

In 1976, Carter "won" the caucuses and put Iowa on the map, but only a few reporters were covering it. By now, the press corps has increased in size and its scope is much bigger. Now candidates must do well in Iowa to do well anywhere else. It snowballed into something.

The media game has just changed immensely. Technology has changed it. As technology gets smaller, its impact gets bigger. The technology is mobile enough that you could go out, spend time with a candidate getting a story, and produce the story immediately. Reporters are enabled by this ever-advancing technology. They don't need eight people—a whole crew—to cover the candidate. Now it's people who do text, podcasts, videos, and internet stuff.

This changes campaign events as well. The crowds are bigger. Much too big for a church basement. You need a hall, an event center to do bigger events, but all that networks need is one reporter.

Journalism is much more contentious now than it used to be. Candidates used to be able to come out to Iowa and try out their stand on issues. C-SPAN makes it possible for what is said in Iowa to be heard all over the country. A candidate can no longer say one thing in one place and another thing in another. Everybody is on record all the time.

They're All Dicks in Iowa
Mark Siegel

It is difficult to remember how cigarette smoking used to dominate American life. Even after smoking was declared carcinogenic and was so labeled on cigarette packs, there were few restrictions and bans on smoking in public places. Even in sports arenas smoking was rampant, casting a haze over the stands.

The 1976 Democratic National Convention was held in Madison Square Garden in New York City, and I served as the DNC's executive director and the convention's political director. I positioned my family in prime VIP seats. During one session my grandfather-in-law Sam Sarna started screaming at the woman next to him, "Lady, you're burning me up." The woman left. She was Lauren Bacall.

The 1980 Democratic National Convention was once again held at Madison Square Garden. I was employed by CBS to be Walter Cronkite's political consultant and convention spotter. I had a small booth directly underneath Cronkite's set, and a live mike connected us. One of my jobs was to keep streaming political commentary to Cronkite at all times, a nonstop monologue that he would occasionally pick up and mimic when he ran dry of other things to say during the gavel-to-gavel coverage. Cronkite was a wonderful person to work with. He was kind and inquisitive, with no pretensions or airs. I was amazed and delighted that he didn't treat me like staff, but rather like a colleague.

I had been the director of the Draft Kennedy movement in 1979 through 1980 and was close to the senator and his staff. One of his advance men on the campaign, Mark Brand, had joined my firm but continued to do advance work for the Kennedy campaign at the national convention.

The 1980 primary season between President Jimmy Carter and Senator Edward Kennedy began with a strong and surprising Carter victory in the first caucus state, Iowa. The campaign alternated between Carter and Kennedy primary victories with Carter capturing the South and Kennedy winning big states like California and New York. Coming into the convention Carter had a small but clear delegate edge.

The Kennedy campaign made a final push to change the delegate balance by a proposed rule change that would free all delegates to vote their conscience, irrespective of how and to whom they were pledged. It was a desperate gamble in the hopes that many of the liberal and labor Carter delegates would switch to Kennedy if they were allowed to. On the first night of the convention, when the rules were to be adopted, the proposed rule change was put to a vote. It was the first and most decisive roll call of the 1980 Democratic National Convention. If Kennedy lost the proposed rule change, he would withdraw his candidacy.

As part of Mark Brand's advance teamwork for the Kennedy campaign, he was put in charge of Senator Kennedy's three children. There was a logistical and medical problem: the senator's youngest child, thirteen-year-old Patrick Kennedy, was asthmatic. Madison Square Garden was permeated with cigarette and cigar smoke. Smoke literally wafted across the stands and up to the Garden's ceiling. Young Patrick could not be exposed to that kind of smoke because of his asthma, and Brand asked me as a favor if Patrick could join me in my little booth.

I, of course agreed, even though my booth was tiny. It was so small that my desk and chair took up the entire space of the booth. The only way Patrick could be with me was if he literally sat on my lap. Brand brought Patrick to me and positioned the boy on my lap. I explained what was about to take place and what my role was at the convention.

Minutes before rule floor fight was to begin, Cronkite went on the air live. I began my litany of nonstop analysis and pointing out interesting developments on the floor and political color. Patrick asked who I was talking to, and I whispered "Walter Cronkite." Patrick yanked my headset off my head and screamed into the microphone, "Hey Walter, how's it going?"

I grabbed the kid and put my headset back on my head and warned him that he could not disrupt my job, and he could not talk into the mike. He said, "But it's Walter Cronkite," and I responded, "Especially because it's Walter Cronkite."

The roll call began with Alabama. The tally was not looking good for Senator Kennedy. And then Dorothy Bush, the secretary of the Democratic National Convention, called for the vote for the state of Iowa. Iowa, which had been won by Carter, cast a majority vote against the rule change, consistent with the Carter position.

At that point thirteen-year-old Patrick Kennedy once again ripped my headset off my head and screamed into the microphone, "Walter, they're all dicks in Iowa."

I said, "Okay, that's it! I warned you. Get out." I opened my booth's door. Brand was standing there. I told Brand that the kid was out of control, and I was throwing him out of my booth.

He said, "But Mark, you can't, he'll die in this smoke."

I said, "Good."

Brand later told me that when he relayed to Senator Kennedy what happened. Kennedy laughed.

Little Patrick Kennedy was elected as congressman from Rhode Island in 1995 and served until 2009.

Momentum
Bill Hershey

In 1992, I covered the Clinton-Gore bus trip, right after the Democratic National Convention in New York City. It was the most interesting, sustained experience I have ever had as a reporter.

I think the Clinton campaign made it up as they went along. They had a general idea, but they didn't really know what was going to happen. I remember getting on the bus in New York City, with George Stephanopoulos standing by the side of the bus as a crowd of people got on board.

Then the trip took off. Clinton was long-winded, but he was a terrific retail campaigner. The bus trip picked up momentum at every stop. We were driving through these rural parts of the states on the freeways. There would be people standing up along the highway holding candles. It was just a continuous line—you couldn't see the end of it.

That's where I learned that when you're covering politics, whenever you get the chance to eat or go to the bathroom, you do it. Because I kept thinking, I'll eat when we get done for the day. Well, Clinton just fed off himself and the crowds. The more places we went, the more places he wanted to go.

I remember coming into Hershey, Pennsylvania. It was after midnight, and it was like a scene out of a novel, *The Last Hurrah*. All these people, candles, and cheering in the town square—and Clinton is just up here, just going on and on. The enthusiasm was contagious.

At another stop, I wanted to see Clinton work the rope line, shaking hands with people. So, I went into the crowd. He didn't know I was a reporter. I had this Detroit Pistons cap on because I was a big Pistons fan. Clinton looked at me like I was the only person in the world, and he said to me, "That's a great cap." It was impressive.

We were at a rest stop on the interstate with Clinton and Gore, and they were throwing around footballs. They wanted to be like the Kennedys. And they had a little bit of that image: two young, idealistic candidates and their smart, engaged wives. It was a great start for the campaign.

A similar experience to the Clinton bus trip, but a little less intense, was when John McCain was running against George W. Bush for the Republican presidential nomination in 2000.

I went up to Michigan to cover the primary because Governor John Engler had endorsed Bush, and the expectation was that Engler would push Bush over the top. I knew a lot of Michigan school teachers, and they hated John Engler. I knew they were going to vote in the Republican primary to spite Engler. It was perfect for McCain.

It was like with Clinton in 1992. The more places McCain went, the more places he wanted to go. He just caught fire; you could feel the momentum growing. He loved the idea of being the underdog, and he played it up. Reporters liked McCain because he was so available—and he actually answered questions. There was a sense of something new and different. It was a great boost for his campaign.

Knowing How to Laugh
Corey Busch

George Moscone defined California liberalism in the 1960s and 1970s. In the state legislature and as mayor of San Francisco, he tirelessly worked for the poor, the excluded, and the marginalized.

In 1974, George launched a campaign for governor of California. His main opponent was Jerry Brown, whose name recognition as the son of a very popular former governor simply could not be beat in the Democratic primary (and who would eventually be elected California governor four times).

George dropped out of the race when one of his chief financial backers told him, "George, I love you, but giving money to you at this point is like packing hay for a dead horse."

George laughed at that description of the state of his campaign—he had a great sense of humor.

During that short-lived 1974 gubernatorial campaign, I traveled throughout the state with him. He was indefatigable as a campaigner. He loved people, and he loved retail politics.

On one particularly hot day, we went to a barrio in Saticoy in Ventura County. It was well over a hundred degrees and the campaign event was outside on what seemed like a Texas plain in the dustbowl. The place was packed. George stopped to speak with each and every person there. The desperation on the faces of the people who came to see him is etched in my mind.

While George shook hands and spent time with the people, I did what I do best: eat. The food was simply delicious. It was all homemade and brought to the event as though it was a potluck.

We spent over two hours in the heat and the dust, and by the time we left to return home, we were both exhausted, dripping in sweat—our shirts were soaked through—and our faces were covered with grime.

We got in the car and George looked over at me and said, "Busch, just once we're going to run a campaign for the uptrodden!"

If you're going to make your living in political campaigns, it helps a lot to work with someone who knows how to laugh.

The Vision Thing
Rick Silver

When we were first starting in the political consulting business, one of our methods of operation was to get inside information from our clients. We wanted to get a sense of their vision, what they wanted to accomplish.

We would always ask this question, "All right, it's a hundred years in the future. You're gone. What's on your tombstone? What do you want to be remembered for? What's that thing you want to accomplish that really stands out and passes the test of time?"

We had a very local race with a good old boy running for sheriff. He heard that question and he got that kind of scowl on his face—not mad, just really confused.

His response was, "I really like billboards. I don't need tombstones. I'd rather have billboards."

I will never forget that response.

Hombre of Enchantment
John Polidori

In 2003, I was working as a political staff guy for the National Education Association (NEA), and my boss, Ken MacGregor, sent me to Santa Fe, New Mexico, to check out the new governor, Bill Richardson, who was making good on his promise to enact a new public employee collective bargaining law.

Upon arrival, our NEA-New Mexico's lobbyist, Charles Bowyer, ushered me to a meeting with Richardson. We anticipated discussion about any loose ends in the bargaining bill. But the "Guv" surfaced a different agenda: a referendum to amend the state's constitution.

"I need you," he announced, face alit with his trademark 'watch this' grin, "We're going to raise teachers' salaries."

Then looking at me, he said: "I hear you know how to do these things."

"Two quick thoughts, Governor," I replied. "Determining the best time to run the election and the actual question wording." I am figuring that he was pointing toward the 2004 election to give us the time to lay it all out.

He laughed—more or less. As I was to learn, that was the classic Richardson "murmur."

"That's done," he replied, "It will be this September 23rd."

When I asked about the amendment wording and requisite opinion research, he wryly remarked: "That's why you're here."

I got back to the office and called my boss. He roared with laughter, "You'll love Santa Fe. Remember, this guy may run for president someday. Don't screw up." (Richardson did run for the Democratic presidential nomination in 2008).

My next call was to my wife, Eva, who had just arrived, unpacked, and finished setting up our new apartment in Denver, Colorado.

"Honey, you're going to love it! I just got reassigned to Santa Fe."

Laughter followed...then a gentle click.

Later that day, I met with Dave Contarino, the chief of staff to the Guv (a fellow one-time Massachusetts guy).

Laughing as I entered his office, his first words were: "I think we've got you the use of the lieutenant governor's casita. Your wife will love it."

He'd never met Eva but demonstrated an intuitive feel for the DTI (Domestic Tranquility Index).

A bonus of working in the "land of enchantment": I did get to wear cowboy boots and jeans every day.

Contarino and the campaign manager, Amanda Cooper, gifted me right off (remember, this was 2003) with a laminated folding map of the state, plus a list of favorite New Mexico "do's, don'ts and must-knows": the difference between Spanish Americans and Mexican Americans; the best natural hot springs; the autumn hot air balloon festival; the state's culinary dividing line—red or green chili; the finest panoramic views: the vast array of Indigenous Peoples; and to remain cognizant of New Mexico's great irony: so much poverty amidst so much beauty.

There are referenda questions to change statutes and then there are amendments to a state constitution. The former could come and go, the latter are like changing marriage vows.

The Guv's first state constitutional amendment simply proposed to create a cabinet-level state Department of Education headed by a secretary of education appointed by the governor. This idea was all about effectiveness: get rid of massive bureaucratic political patronage in education so the governor could hold education officials accountable.

The Guv's second amendment, however, proposed changing the annual disbursement from the state's "Permanent Fund"—a massive trust fund (then $6 billion, now over $13 billion) that received royalties from oil, gas, and grazing leases on public lands, courtesy of New Mexico's statehood act. The governor wanted to increase the annual payout and dedicate it to raising teacher salaries.

Earned media being the key, I was sent on mission to explain these amendments to the media so it could convey accurate information to voters. Gilbert Gallegos, the governor's deputy press secretary, and I did two week-long treks to the four corners of New Mexico. Back and forth to all kinds of media outlets from Silver City to Farmington to Gallup and, of course, to Roswell and Alamogordo: Radio, television, newspapers (daily and weekly), reporters, editorial boards, talk shows, and point-counterpoint on TV and radio news.

At the one-month mark, we began the first of two statewide gubernatorial barnstorming tours using the state airplane (when we weren't in the Guv's Chevy Suburban with him directing the security detail to hurry up—favorite speeds being in the 80–90 mph range, often on "time-saving" two-lane county roads and ranch dirt road short cuts).

On the first plane ride, I handed him the stock speech: six pages of talking points with sound bites.

Farmington, stop one: Republican part of the state; oil and gas lands; local radio and TV at a community college auditorium; about seventy-five people there; decent midweek crowd. The Guv opens the notebook, but barely uses the notes. He just wings it in his trademark folksy kind of way, missing the key points and the linkage to accountability. WTF. I'm looking at Contarino in the back of the room, he just shrugs. He's seen the act before.

We get back into the plane. The Guv directs me to the seat across from him. "How'd I do?" Gulp. His accompanying look could have sliced me. I just smiled. He doesn't say another word. Then he quickly pages through the notebook for maybe about two minutes, then closes it and looks out the window. We get to the next stop. He gets out, walks in, and runs the entire script without missing a beat—and never opened the notebook.

I turn to Contarino and before I could say a word, he whispers coyly to me: "You didn't know?" He held up his hands as if holding a camera and depressing an index finger, "Click."

Back on the plane, the Guv sarcastically says: "How the hell did I do this time?" I started to compliment him, but he had already opened the notebook and was crumpling each sheet up into a ball and tossing them at me one at a time. Then he closed his eyes and took a cat nap.

Meanwhile, the Guv had convinced Republican U.S. senator Pete Domenici to star in our last statewide ad, looking straight to camera, about the fiscal soundness of the funding amendment. Pete was deservedly respected as a fiscal conservative, and as a fair, common-sense guy as well. It was a pure Richardson move: enlist the would-be opposition. Rumors continue to this day on what deal it took to get this done.

Both amendments were adopted. The secretary of education amendment rolled by 10 percent. As for the increased payout from the permanent fund to raise teacher salaries? It rolled a 195-vote win out of 184,201 votes cast. When I asked the Guv about the potential for a recount, I got that smug grunt-laugh of his. "No, (stupid), we certify results quickly here."

Richardson, a rabid Yankee admirer, knowing that I was a big Red Sox fan, had promised me during the campaign that if we won, he'd gift me the Red Sox jacket that Pedro Martinez had given him. To this day, Contarino, another Red Sox zealot, hangs the jacket in his office closet.

Distaff Difference
Celinda Lake

Voters are getting used to the idea of women having multiple roles, both traditional and nontraditional. They admire women who have been entrepreneurs, fighter pilots, or who have run a construction company. Nontraditional experiences keep women candidates from being perceived as too liberal. Voters don't think a woman Democratic candidate fighter pilot is a socialist; they don't think that women business owners are socialists, either. Multiple roles mix up the ideological spectrum.

But there are still problems with single women candidates. It used to be easier to run as a single woman than it is today. It used to be that the biggest problem single women had was the assumption they were lesbian. One of the ways to deal with that perception was to put children in photos and ads. There was a study done by the Ford Family Foundation that looked at the family issue involving candidates. They found that single moms did a lot better than single women at the ballot box.

Tammy Duckworth was a special case because she was a disabled veteran. She was elected to the U.S. House of Representatives and the U.S. Senate from Illinois. Then there's Tammy Baldwin, who is openly lesbian. She was elected in the U.S. House and U.S. Senate from Wisconsin.

Veterans are testing well these days now—male or female. Voters believe veterans have integrity and don't think of them as particularly left or right. Evangelists were critical of Duckworth when she had a baby at age fifty. But she was the incumbent. It's easier as an incumbent because people think, "I know you, and you've done a good job. I'm not going to fire you just because you had a baby." For an incumbent who has a child, people think, "She's already done so much and the fact that she survived losing her legs was a strong positive."

However, if she had been the mother of a young child when she was first running, I think it would have been a lot harder. Voters say they want tough women candidates, but they often don't like them when they are tough.

It's interesting to observe different ways to show toughness that make voters comfortable. There was a transgender woman who ran for state legislature in Oklahoma. She told hysterical stories. She was a police officer and transitioned her gender status as a police officer. She was told "Get voters to know you. You must go door to door and talk to voters." Her advisers had to tell her to not knock on the door like a police officer. "Maybe tap a little less and stand a little away from the door." She said, "All my training says to rap on the door and step aside. They said, 'You're a candidate now, not a police officer.'"

A contrast is Jody Ernst, a Republican U.S. senator from Iowa. The troops in her unit said, "She was a tough leader who really watched out for us." That endorsement just went off the charts. Another positive was when she said, "I grew up on a farm. I know how to castrate hogs." Such a mix of nontraditional and traditional backgrounds are traits that voters are good with.

You're Not Going to Believe This
Lincoln Mitchell

In 2001, I was the general consultant on several New York City races. The night before the primary, I had been working at the campaign headquarters of a City Council candidate named Alan J. Gerson. Alan was in a tough race, but we thought he had a good chance of winning. His district was in lower Manhattan and included Chinatown, Little Italy, SoHo, Tribeca, Wall Street, much of Greenwich Village, and several other neighborhoods. It was a fun district in which to do a campaign—not least because of the great restaurants.

Alan had been born and raised in the district and had extremely strong ties to much of the political and community leadership in the area. He was not always slick and polished but was smart and sincere. However, it was a very competitive race. One candidate outspent us by a factor of at least three to one. Another won the endorsement of the *New York Times,* which was hugely influential in the white liberal areas of the district, while several Chinese American candidates were likely to pull more votes out of Chinatown than Alan.

Our strategy was to compete everywhere and win big in a handful of election districts in the Village, SoHo, and Tribeca. One place we expected to do well was Battery Park City, a mostly middle-class housing development on the southwestern corner of the island. We had a wonderful coordinator for that area named Robin who lived there and seemed to know all the residents. She was planning to spend Election Day (a holiday in New York) with her school-age daughter at the polling place for Battery Park City asking her friends and neighbors to vote for Alan.

I ended up working very late the night before the election and managed to get two hours of sleep at a desk in the campaign office before getting up for the morning rush. By about 8:30 am, my intern and I had gotten everybody out on the street, to subway stops, school drop-offs and the like.

I was resting for a few minutes when I heard an extremely loud noise. A few minutes later, one of Alan's volunteers ran upstairs saying something about an attack and that we needed to get out. I got him to calm down long enough to tell me that the sound I heard was an airplane hitting the World Trade Center.

Election Day in 2001 was on September 11, and the World Trade Center was part of Alan's district. It was also where people who lived in Battery Park City voted because there was a polling place in the basement of the World Trade Center. Maybe it was the lack of sleep or just the strangeness of the moment, but within minutes I picked up the phone and called the Board of Elections.

I got somebody I knew on the phone and said, "You're not going to believe this, but an airplane just hit the World Trade Center, and I want to make sure that people will still be allowed to vote in the basement, and that they won't lose their right to vote." At that time, no one realized how severe the loss of life would be. The person on the other end of the phone after asking me to slow down and explain several times, simply said "hold on." He didn't put me on hold, but simply put the phone down. I could hear him take a few steps and then gasp. I presumed he had looked out the window and seen what had happened. He then returned to the phone and said, "I got to call you back."

Within hours the election was canceled.

A few hours later, as I was making my way home on foot, I thought of Robin and her daughter who probably had been in the World Trade Center when the planes hit, so I called Robin and got her voicemail. I left a message and said, "Something terrible has happened. Please call and let me know if you are okay." I did not hear back from her for a few days, but eventually she thanked me for the call, and said both she and her daughter were fine.

The primary was postponed until September 25. Robin was back volunteering for the new Election Day, but the polling place had been moved.

We did very well in those Battery Park City election districts, and Alan won the race.

Two Point Boy!
Phil Noble

In 1992, a Republican congressman named Tommy Hartnett was running against the long-serving U.S. senator Fritz Hollings in South Carolina.

My office was across the street from Senator Hollings local office, and one day, I got a call from Hollings's office staff saying, "The senator would like to talk with you." I told them that I've been out running and that I was all smelly, sweaty, and wearing gym shorts—and unless it was something pressing, I'd come see him the next day. They said, "No, he wants to come over to see you right now." I said, "Okay."

So, Senator Hollings comes over to my office. We had a little minimal chitchat, and then he says, "I'm running against Hartnett this year, and they tell me you're the guy who knows more about opposition research than anyone else. Would you do the research for my campaign?"

Of course, I said, "Yes, sir."

He had finished everything he wanted to say in about three minutes, and he knew it would be sort of impolite to just get up and leave, so he asked me, "What do you think about the race?"

I said, "Well, Senator, I'm a voter here, so why should I vote for you? "

"Well, I'm up in Washington, D.C.," he starts, "We balanced the trade deficit, but the Chinese are eating our lunch." He just went on and on and on about the

Gramm-Rudman-Hollings bill, how he was chairman of this and that committee, and all sorts of Washington stuff.

There was a clock behind him, and I watched the second hand go round and round until finally he stopped his filibuster, and said, "That's it, what do you think about it?"

I said, "Senator, do you want me to tell you the truth?" I thought I'd earned the right to ask him that since I had just agreed to do a ton of research for him, and I was a little pissed as he didn't say anything about my getting paid.

He stammered a bit and dismissively said, "Yeah, yeah, yeah."

"Senator, you have just talked for eight and a half minutes," I said, "and you didn't say the word *education*, which is the most important thing to me. And I'm a big environmentalist and you didn't say anything about the environment. And you didn't say anything about a whole host of issues that I and a lot of people in South Carolina care about."

As I was going down the list, I could tell he was getting madder and madder—but I decided to just go all in.

"Honestly, Senator, you're out of touch. I think Tommy Hartnett will give you a hell of a race. I don't know if you're going to win or lose, but I think it's going to be a two-point race."

"Two points," he exploded. "You think that dumb SOB is going to get within two points of me!" Hollings shouted. "Well, you're supposed to be smart—two points! You're full of crap!" "Two points! Two points!"

He went on like that in a mild rage for a minute or so, then abruptly got up and left in a huff.

I did the research, which largely validated what I had said, and I gave it to his campaign manager. I didn't want to brief him in person as I knew how he would respond—it would not be pretty. Two or three times during the campaign season,

I'd see him at various political events, and he'd always sneer at me, "There's my two-point boy, two points, huh!"

I didn't say a word.

Well, it was a real close election, but Hollings won—with 50.07%.

One of Hollings's longtime supporters was a good friend of mine, and he always had a New Year's Eve party. The Hollings and I were regulars. At the party that year, I saw him across the way several times during the evening. When he saw me, I just politely nodded to him; he did not respond. For the next two or three hours we would periodically make eye contact—but neither one of us said a word or moved to speak to the other. I could tell that every time he saw me, it was more and more unsettling to him.

Just after midnight, after he had more than a few glasses of New Year's cheer, suddenly he walked across the room to where I was standing, stood a foot from me and looked me right in the eye and said, "Noble, I'ma gonna say this once and only once. You was right, and I was wrong. I was a goddamn fool."

He turned and walked away in a hurry like he had somewhere to go.

I really appreciated what he said because I knew just how hard it was for him to say it. Our mutual friend was standing nearby and overhead what Hollings said. My friend leaned over and said, "I have known Fritz for nearly fifty years, and that's the first time I ever heard him apologize about anything."

Neither Hollings nor I ever mentioned it again.

From 2 to 1 to Just 2 Points Down
John Zogby

In 1996, a local lawyer had already tried three times to be elected as a city court judge and never exceed 20 percent of the two-candidate vote.

"I want to try it again," he told me.

He wanted a poll and needed to know the right kind of messaging he would need to defeat a Republican incumbent who happened to be very popular. After ascertaining some key facts, I agreed to draft a survey.

In a poll that focused on messaging, the key rule is to ask the "horse race" questions up front and then collect basic data on the favorable/unfavorable ratio of both candidates. The lawyer was down two to one to the incumbent judge.

But then the task is to test the wording of messages and responses to issues or situations to discover whether each would make the respondent more likely or less likely to vote for the candidate.

A key piece of information that needed to be tested was that the incumbent was sixty-eight years old, and there was mandatory retirement for all judges at age seventy throughout New York State. So, we posed this issue three distinct ways. First, that at age sixty-eight, the sitting judge would be forced to retire in two years and not be able to finish a ten-year term. Second, that his age meant that he would have to step down. And third, simply that he would not complete his full term.

The third message was working well, with voters saying three to one that they would be more likely to support his opponent. It worked because we did not use age, something we discovered would be unfair, perhaps even mean, and clearly turned off voters over sixty-five years of age—who vote in large numbers.

After the message tests, we posed the horse race question again, and this time our guy was down by only two percentage points, 48 percent to 46 percent.

I would like to be able to tell you that he won, but he lost by a two-point margin, 51 percent to 49 percent—but he did a hell of a lot better than the three previous runs.

Hernias and Back Pain
Hank Sheinkopf

In the 1980s, political consultant Matt Reese created a business model that the Harvard Business School would have really liked: full service. What Reese figured out was that if you tied television time buying to the polling, you'd never have a bad day. Not one dime should be left behind.

But what consultants didn't know how to do then was manage a business. People in political consulting in that era were not businesspeople. Because you were always on the road, you had to take personal computers that were so heavy they'd give you a hernia and back pain. Most of us got back pains later in life because we carried them in a bag over our shoulders. And in the same bag was underwear, socks, shaving gear, and a book. No checked baggage. You could run to catch your plane faster. There were no easy-to-get American Express cards; you'd take a Mastercard if you were lucky. There were no cell phones, so you'd take an AT&T credit card.

It was a whole different thing than it is now. Jerry Austin, my business partner at the time, and I went to California to see someone. We had set up the appointment a couple of days before, and we reinforced it with an office call to make sure it was still on. They didn't show. It happened often.

Our business really changed in the mid-1990's. You had to be a salesman and you had to be a genius. The competition increased and approval by Washington-based political bureaucrats could mean you ate, or if they didn't like you, you starved.

Then there was the rise of regional consultants who made it less likely to get work if you weren't from a particular state. Why would candidates hire you when they could hire a local consultant that might be as good? It saved the candidates money, and it created a new echo chamber for criticism. There were always players in states like Texas, Florida, and California that no one had ever heard outside of those states. They made lots of money and they never left home. No matter how smart you were, how good you were as a salesperson, or how good your work was, you weren't going to get work in the state.

"Aren't they wonderful?" was a phrase said about you by someone sitting at a desk in an office building, whose main job had been smiling at the candidates they worked for.

Never a Politician

Bill Fletcher

I was working for the Senate Democratic caucus in the Florida legislature in 1990. The leadership wanted to target a Republican incumbent named Tim Deratany. He was the chairman of the powerful Senate finance committee. Typically, you can't beat somebody in leadership, especially somebody in finance leadership, because of their connections.

The first step was to recruit a good candidate. We did a lot of "AB" testing on the question "Would you prefer a candidate with this or prefer a candidate with that?" Our pollster, Jim Kitchens, came back and told us what we needed was a woman who has a little government experience, but not in the government.

So, we start running traps, looking to recruit such a candidate. Eventually, we found a woman named Patsy Ann Kurth. She was a realtor and had served on a government board of some kind—so she had a little government experience but was in the private sector. She was married and had a beautiful daughter.

As we talked with her, we were trying to figure out if she could raise the money needed to win the race.

She was so nonpolitical that she said, "Well, I don't know if it will matter or not, but Dick Gephardt is my cousin."

We said, "THE Dick Gephardt?"

She said, "Yeah. Do you think he could help me raise money?"

Oh, sure, we thought he might be able to help raise a few dollars! So, she became our candidate against Tim Deratany.

The opposition research boys went to work and found an unusual situation involving the incumbent.

State legislators in Florida are part-time, and they can hold other jobs. Deratany had a job with a community college that was paying him $80,000 a year. It turns out the incumbent's finance connections appeared to have paid off—literally.

After the Challenger space shuttle exploded, Florida issued a specialty license plate commemorating the astronauts that were killed. It had an extra $10 fee to raise a couple of million dollars to build a memorial for the astronauts. It was a big hometown deal in Deratany's district, which included the Kennedy Space Center.

Well, it turned out that everybody in Florida had to have one of those license plates. It unexpectedly raised something like $30 million dollars. Suddenly, there's this giant pot of money just sitting there. Deratany pushed through a bipartisan bill to spend much of this money for grants to colleges and universities around the state to fund engineering and flight safety programs—a very appropriate thing.

Deratany then got several millions of these dollars sent to the local community college—which then put him put on the payroll for $80,000 a year. I'm not saying it was a "no show" job, but let's just say that it didn't pass the smell test.

I made a campaign spot with the archival footage of the Challenger as it took off, and a voiceover saying that Tim Deratany had converted money meant for the Challenger astronauts memorial to a big salary for himself.

I sent the spot to Patsy. To her credit, it made her weep. She started crying because she said it was just too mean. She was a political novice we had brought into campaign combat. She was just not ready for the level of malice required to defeat a strong incumbent like Tim Deratany. She refused to use the television ad.

Then, Deratany's campaign did an attack that went after Patsy's family. She changed her mind about using the ad, wisely insisting I remove the explosion, just freezing the video right before it exploded.

The spot was a sensation, even making national news. Patsy and her ragtag band of volunteers ran a great grassroots campaign, and the Senate caucus ran the television ad in support of her candidacy. Patsy won the race, but only by about two percentage points.

Senator Kurth served with distinction in the state legislature for many years, but she never became a politician—because she wasn't one to start with.

Check with the Post Office
Gerry Tyson

In 1973, we were working for Houston mayoral candidate (and future mayor) Fred Hofheinz in a runoff against a well-financed candidate whose campaign was being managed by consultant Matt Reese.

As we planned our phone and mail Get Out the Vote (GOTV) operation, we took our mail pieces to the postal service's permits section for approval, a standard practice in all our campaigns. Previewing mail pieces with these officials gives them an opportunity to tell us if they found problems with what we were mailing. In this case, the person in charge of approving mailers objected to our use of the word "telegram" on the outside of the piece, despite the term being in the public domain, not trademarked, and we had received approval for its use in other postal regions.

So, we substituted the suggested term "Electo-Gram" and had our pieces printed for mailing.

As we were visiting the mail house during final production, I noticed a discarded piece of mail labeled "Telegram" on the production room floor, so I picked it up, fearing something had gone wrong with our mail. However, I saw that the piece was one being produced for our runoff opponent, so I put it in my pocket as we continued the tour.

Once we got back to the Hofheinz headquarters, we told the campaign manager what we had found as well as what the postal permit office had told us about the banned use of the word "telegram." Waiting until we thought our opponent probably had delivered his "telegrams" to the post office just before Election Day, we revisited the permits office and pointed out that our opponent was mailing a piece carrying the term "Telegram" that we had been forbidden to use.

As a result of our protest, our opponent's 95,000 pieces of GOTV mail were NOT mailed. We won the runoff by approximately 1,200 votes.

The lesson of this story is to always make certain the post office will approve your mail piece before you ever finish its design and production. The failure of our opponent to do so probably cost him the election. Furthermore, if you're running a mail house, it's also a good idea to know what the post office will approve or not. In this case, the losing candidate sued the mail house for lack of due diligence, and, as I recall, the mail house went out of business.

The American Way
Bill Fletcher

I learned the power of language and images early in my career. I was working for Joe Haynes, an attorney running for the state legislature in Tennessee.

In 1984, Joe was gerrymandered out his district: his rivals ran a finger up the road to his property and moved him into another district. The Democratic leadership did this right before the qualifying deadline for the election to deter him from running against an entrenched incumbent. When asked about the gerrymandering, the leader arrogantly said, "It's the American way."

In response, Joe and his family moved out of their home into a two-bedroom apartment. In sharp contrast to their suburban home with a pool and lush grounds, the apartment was small, cramped and in need of a coat of paint. He then qualified to run against the incumbent as planned.

That night I wrote a speech for Joe Haynes entitled "The American Way." I told the story of Joe growing up on a farm in Castilian Springs, Tennessee, becoming an engineer at the University of Tennessee, going to work for the DuPont plant in Old Hickory, going to law school at night, and raising a family. After each biographical point, Joe would say, "That is the American Way."

In those days, speeches still mattered. Joe made that speech to civic clubs, churches, and anywhere he could gather a small audience. We noticed that heads would begin nodding as he explained how the political bosses had removed him from the district where he lived and practiced law. It was as if we were seeing people decide, "I'll show the bosses what The American Way really is."

"The American Way" became the theme of Joe's campaign. I made TV commercials and developed direct mail for him, all based on The American Way theme. He shocked the political establishment and won a very challenging race.

Joe had a long career as a state senator. Eventually, he became the chairman of the Senate Democratic Caucus—the same group that had gerrymandered him out of his district.

There will always be hijinks in campaigns because there are human beings involved. But I learned a powerful lesson in this campaign and others: the power of harnessing language and images in the pursuit of high ideals like "The American Way."

I speak to college classes regularly, and I know that political consultants are held in low regard. Fortunately, I'm missing a gene, and I've never cared what other people think. It's a gift and a curse.

But I say this: what we do in political consulting is important because our work determines who governs the Republic. It determines who holds the offices and who has the power. It is a responsibility that I've always taken very, very seriously. It's not my job to have every great idea. It's my job to recognize one when I see it. We tell big stories that matter to people that offer them choices and give them a voice. This is The American Way.

I always tell these young people, "You can go chase dollars if you want to, but if you want to be at the ground level of the democratic experience in the United States of America, the only place you can get that is in electoral politics."

This is why I've walked past millions of dollars in lobbying fees.

I don't want to give other people's money to politicians and ask them to do things. I don't like to lobby. I don't enjoy it.

I want to take politicians' money and help teach them what to do to win the support of voters.

It is a lot of fun. I enjoy it. It is very satisfying.

Joe Haynes remained my client for twenty years until he retired from the Tennessee state senate. Until the day he died, if you went into his law office in Goodlettsville, Tennessee, you would have seen the framed original speech, "The American Way," with his notes and edits scribbled in the margins.

That is the power of language.

That is The American Way.

Maxed Out and None the Wiser
Les Francis

As the 1972 presidential election approached, I became enamored with the likely candidacy of New York's Mayor John V. Lindsay. Lindsay, a former liberal Republican member of Congress from New York's so-called Silk Stocking district in Manhattan, switched parties to run for the Democratic presidential nomination (his views were not welcome in the increasingly conservative GOP).

I admit I was drawn by his Kennedy-style charisma and his progressive views on domestic issues, particularly civil rights. His opposition to the war in Vietnam was also important to me. Finally, being mayor of New York City may be, behind the presidency, the toughest elected job in America, and I liked the idea of having someone representing urban America in the White House.

Not insignificant in my calculations, as well, was the fact that my boss, Congressman Norman Mineta, had become a good friend and ally of Lindsay's through their work together on the Legislative Action Committee of the U.S. Conference of Mayors. Norm was likely to play a key role in any Lindsay campaign or administration.

Sure enough, when Lindsay announced his candidacy in early 1972, Norm was named as a national cochair of the campaign. Norm, in turn, requested that the campaign hire me to help coordinate the California effort. I arranged to take a leave of absence from my job as executive director of the Orange Unified Education

Association—a leave which was made all the more welcome because of an internecine war that was gripping the California Teachers Association (CTA) at the time—and hit the road for Lindsay.

As Northern California Field Director, my job was to first recruit volunteers and supporters to attend congressional district caucuses which would select Lindsay delegates to the national convention. My second and much more amorphous job was to create a Lindsay organizational presence throughout the northern three-quarters of the state, from Bakersfield to the Oregon border, including the vote-rich Bay Area and the more sparsely populated great Central Valley. But I wasn't *just* the Director of the Northern California field operation, I was *the* Northern California Field Operation.

All I had to do the job was my own car, my personal credit card, and former Speaker of the California State Assembly Jesse Unruh's Christmas card list (which was maintained on 3 x 5 index cards stored in a shoebox in alphabetical order by last name). I never knew exactly how Unruh's list found its way to the Lindsay campaign, but it did. I became its custodian and temporary beneficiary.

I crisscrossed Northern California, recruiting adherents as best I could, working out of the Northern California headquarters on San Francisco's Kearney Street. I resided, when not on the road, at my parents' home in San Jose some fifty miles to the south of San Francisco, which meant long days and long commutes.

As I traveled the state, I would arrive in Fresno, Modesto, Monterey, or wherever, and check into a Holiday Inn, pull out the shoebox of Jess Unruh's index cards, go through all several hundred, and find those in the same geographic area. I would then turn to the local phone book and attach phone numbers to the names and addresses. Then I would begin making cold calls to folks. I'd introduce myself and explain the purpose of my call. The response rate was, as one might expect, underwhelming! It was, obviously, long before computers and associated software that would have cut hours of work down to seconds.

But more importantly, I quickly came to realize that almost everywhere I went the campaign of South Dakota senator George McGovern had already been there. In fact, with few exceptions, he had already enlisted the first-string organizers from labor, the anti-war movement, the environmentalists, and other elements of the activist Democratic base in the state. It was an early indication of McGovern's strength, which eventually propelled him to the party's presidential nomination that summer.

The Lindsay presidential campaign lasted for only a couple of months (Lindsay dropped out after a disastrous showing in the Wisconsin primary), but it was an invaluable experience for me. It broadened my network of contacts among Democrats in California, while at the same time helping me build a reputation as an effective political organizer.

When the Lindsay campaign ended, a couple of key people in CTA wanted me to return to Orange County as a member of the state staff rather than as a local executive director. That was also my strong preference. However, CTA's then statewide executive director, Jack Rees, was never too high on me. He thought of me as both too radical (in terms of collective bargaining and teacher advocacy) and as way too political (he wanted CTA's connection to politics to be tightly controlled by him and centralized in his office). I was convinced that Jack was comfortable with CTA's historic—if unofficial—ties to the Republican Party (hard to believe now, I know). I think that he saw my own political network, which was entirely within the Democratic Party, as an unwelcome development at best and a threat at worst.

So, when Rees interviewed me for the job in Orange County. Jack said he would permit my hiring *only* if I pledged to stay out of all political activity, no exceptions. I wanted—no, I needed—the job so badly (those credit card bills from the campaign were overdue!) that I quickly agreed to the stipulation. As a result, I was hired and went about doing my job and living in accordance with Jack Rees's dictum.

Until, that is, Wayne Carruthers, a CTA lobbyist in Sacramento, called and asked me for help in the third state senate district special election campaign. The candidate was Ernie LaCoste, and Barry Wyatt was his campaign manager. Barry had helped me with the Lindsay effort and went on to become one of the Democratic Party's more colorful and effective advance men. He remains a friend to this day. Barry and Wayne wanted me to do a review of the LaCoste campaign and make recommendations as to how it might be given a strategic and organizational boost.

I explained to Wayne that I was under orders from Jack Rees to abstain from all such activity. Wayne assured me that I could come into the district secretly, do the audit he wanted done, and fly back to Orange County, with no one—especially Jack Rees—the wiser. He also said that if Jack somehow learned of my involvement, he (Wayne) would cover for me. Just how he might do that was never explained, but away I went, nevertheless.

However, because my personal credit card was maxed out (thanks to the Lindsay campaign), the only way I could buy an airline ticket or rent a car was to use my CTA credit card. Rather than have an airline ticket which showed me flying from Orange County into Modesto, Stockton, or even Sacramento, I flew to Oakland. I rented an Avis car there and drove to Modesto, where I hooked up with the candidate and Barry Wyatt. We spent the next three days meeting with supporters and volunteers, and attending/participating in various campaign events, including coffees, a parade in Farmville, and an Odd Fellows Pancake breakfast in the picturesque Gold Rush town of Sutter Creek.

It was in Sutter Creek that things went bad.

We arrived in town somewhat late on Saturday evening (the Odd Fellows breakfast was set for Sunday morning). I parked my rental car on the street and checked into the historic and, shall we say, "quaint," Bellotti Hotel. We dumped our bags in our rooms and headed across the street to have a couple of drinks and a late dinner.

About halfway through the meal, a drunk man stumbled into the dining room, and in a way reminiscent of the late comedian Foster Brooks, shouted out: "Ish there annyonne in here whoosh d-d-dr-driving a bluuue D-D-Dodge Poll—arrra?"

I said, "I am."

To which the drunk man replied, "Wellll, yoou'd better come ouside 'cus sommun in a truk jush ba-bac-backed innto it and ripped the shit outta it!"

I jumped up, ran outside and, to my horror, saw a flatbed truck that had backed into the car. The underside of the truck bed was just about an inch shy of the height of the car's hood, so when it backed into the car it literally peeled back a good chunk of the hood like the top of a can of smoked oysters. The truck's driver (no doubt the drunk man who by then had disappeared) had indeed "ripped the shit out of" my rental car—the car on the CTA credit card with a $100 deductible, the car rented in Oakland and wrecked in Sutter Creek.

Thankfully, the campaign gave me enough cash to pay for the car, including the deductible and the airline ticket, so a record of the incident never showed up in CTA's headquarters.

Jack Rees went to his grave a few years later none the wiser.

Data Science
Gerry Tyson

We helped elect Jim Hahn as mayor of Los Angeles in 2001, when he defeated former Assembly Speaker Antonio Villaraigosa. Facing reelection in 2005, Hahn had lost support among voters in two of his 2001 bases—the San Fernando Valley in northwest Los Angeles and the African American community.

As for the San Fernando Valley base, Hahn had strongly opposed a secession movement supported by a significant number of voters in that part of the city. As for African Americans, Hahn had decided not to renew the contract of Police Chief Bernard Parks, an African American, and instead appointed former New York City Police Commissioner Bill Bratton to the position. Parks subsequently was elected to the City Council in 2003 and decided to challenge Hahn in the 2005 mayoral race.

The field of candidates challenging Hahn in 2005 included Parks and Villaraigosa as well as another former Assembly Speaker, Robert Hertzberg, who had represented an Assembly District encompassing a portion of the San Fernando Valley.

Thus, the task facing Hahn was daunting.

Bill Carrick, who was Hahn's chief strategist and media consultant, presented us with a challenging task: how would we identify Hahn supporters in a sub-universe of some 250,000 voters who were indicated by survey research as mostly undecided or split between Hahn and Hertzberg when the funding for phone contacts was severely limited? Polling indicated that if Hahn couldn't beat Hertzberg among these voters, it would be Hertzberg—not Hahn—who would earn a runoff berth along with Villaraigosa.

Our response was to call on Ken Strasma, with whom we had worked in the 2004 Kerry presidential campaign. We drafted a survey instrument that included a Hahn reelect question as well as questions asking respondents which of the candidates they would definitely *not* support. We completed approximately ten thousand random interviews in the target universe and turned the data over to Strasma, who built a Hahn support statistical model as well as an "undecided" model. These models were then used to score the target electorate regarding each voter's likelihood to support Hahn or be undecided.

The universe was divided into quintiles, and we began conducting persuasion identification phone calls in the highest scoring quintile, identifying Hahn supporters. Each day, we would compare the percentage of voters identifying for Hahn with the aggregate score of the voters interviewed that day, and the two numbers tracked closely with each other throughout the calling period. At a point midway through the second-highest quintile, we reached our budget ceiling and turned to the task of mobilizing the Hahn supporters we had identified.

Hahn beat Hertzberg by fewer than seven thousand votes out of more than four hundred thousand total primary votes cast, thus earning the runoff spot against Villaraigosa—a rematch of the 2001 runoff. But Hahn, with little funding and without the support bases he had enjoyed in 2001, lost the 2005 runoff by a substantial margin, 59 to 41 percent. Some observers believe that had Hertzberg been Villaraigosa's runoff opponent, he would have become mayor.

The Carter Connection
Les Francis

Through my friendship with Norman Y. Mineta (going back to my unsuccessful race for the California State Assembly in 1970), I was his chief unofficial political adviser from the time he ran for mayor in 1971 throughout much of his career since. When he was elected to Congress in the post-Watergate election of 1974, he asked me to come to Washington, D.C., and take on the job of administrative assistant (the role we now know as chief of staff).

I was thrilled to do so.

One day in July 1975, Norm was over on the House floor or in a committee meeting elsewhere on the Hill, when into our office walked the former governor of Georgia, Jimmy Carter. Carter and Norm had met during the 1974 campaign, and the former governor and now declared Democratic presidential candidate (at about one percent in the polls), had decided to "drop by" and congratulate Norm on his election as chairman of the Freshman Democratic Caucus.

As the senior staffer in the office, it naturally fell to me to greet Carter, explain Norm's absence, chat for a few minutes about politics and Carter's embryonic presidential campaign. It was a brief and very friendly exchange that Carter ended by saying something like, "I've got to go now, but we're having a little reception tonight at the Sheraton Hotel near National Airport. I'm going to give a brief speech, answer a few questions, and afterwards we can talk some more. It will only cost you $25, so why don't you come by?"

I agreed to do so—and my life was changed forever.

I don't remember a lot of what Carter said exactly that night, either in his speech or in our conversation later. But I do remember that as he spoke, I realized that he was talking about the very same things that pollsters Peter Hart and Pat Caddell had discussed in a private briefing for a few members of Congress and staffers I had attended a few weeks earlier. Jimmy Carter was employing messages that were 100 percent in tune with the polling. Plus, I was greatly impressed, even then, with Carter's humility and genuineness.

I came out of the reception a Carter fan and a truly early supporter.

As the months went by, I watched Carter's campaign, as implausible as it might have seemed to party professionals and Washington pundits, gather more and more political momentum. I made a few more modest contributions (never more than $25 at a time, because that's all I could afford). I also advised friends and associates to pay attention to Carter, that he could go all the way to the Democratic convention and the White House. Most of them just chuckled and reminded me of my work for John Lindsay in the 1972 presidential primaries—about which I had been just as confident.

By the time the 1976 Pennsylvania primary was approaching in late April 1976, Carter had indeed emerged as a major contender for the nomination. He had shown appeal in the Midwest (Iowa) and Northeast (New Hampshire) and had dispatched George Wallace (in the Florida). His volunteer base was very impressive in numbers and impact everywhere they turned up. The race had narrowed, for all intents and purposes, to Carter, Senator Henry "Scoop" Jackson of Washington state, and Arizona Congressman Mo Udall.

Pennsylvania was the showdown state for Carter and Jackson. Whoever survived there was virtually destined to become the centrist alternative to the more liberal Udall. Losing Pennsylvania would either likely end the candidacy of one or the other.

I decided to volunteer my services to the Carter campaign. I called his Pennsylvania manager, Tim Kraft (who I'd never met, but whose reputation as a masterful organizer had impressed me) and told him that I could take ten days of vacation and come to Pennsylvania if he thought I could help. Tim, in the style of a classic organizer, invoked flattery—and probably total bullshit—when he said that he had already heard good things about me and that he would be absolutely delighted to have me come up and help. He said I should come to the headquarters in Philadelphia, and he'd deploy me from there.

I drove to Philly (in my 1976 yellow Audi 100—not exactly good for a union state like Pennsylvania where "Buy American" was an even more compelling cry than "Go Steelers" or "Go Phillies!"). Still, that's what I did. I took with me a young fellow who was an intern in Congressman Jerry Patterson's office who'd also been bitten by the Carter bug. In any event, we met with Kraft in Philadelphia and, after mulling the options, he decided to dispatch us to Washington County, in the southwest corner of the state (between Pittsburgh and West Virginia).

After a very long, late-night drive from one side of the state to the other, we hooked up with Dennis Hils and his wife in Washington, Pennsylvania, who were, as it turned out, *the* Carter organization in the county. We stayed at their farmhouse on the outskirts of town, which also served as our humble headquarters. We had no volunteers, no operation, and no lists. And the primary was ten days away.

We recruited on a nearby college campus (California State College), and we brought Mrs. Carter in for a day of plant gate greetings in the Monongahela Valley. I also arranged for her to drop by at a faculty wives' gathering with author Truman Capote (a truly weird guy) at the college. We were desperate for exposure and would jump at any opportunity to get either the candidate, his wife, or other surrogates in front of any group of voters—no matter how big or small. As I look back on this experience, I marvel at how amateurish it all was!

Given the fact that we had absolutely no people, other than the four of us, I struggled to figure out how we would get the Carter message out.

The answer, it turned out, was found in the fact that the local congressman was retiring. The seat was solidly Democratic, so there was a spirited primary contest for the Democratic congressional nomination—with eleven primary candidates seeking the nomination.

I approached the top three leading candidates and asked each of them if they would include Jimmy Carter on their "slate cards" that would be going out in the mail and via door-to-door canvassing. In those conversations, it is entirely possible that I might have intimated that we—and the by then vaunted Carter volunteer operation—would respond in kind. Each of the three agreed, not knowing of course, that I had conducted the same conversation with all three. In my defense, not one of them ever asked me that question! Nor did any of them ask me the size or capacity of the Carter operation in the county.

To help reinforce the impression such an organization had arrived in Washington County, I ordered five thousand green, black, and white "Jimmy Carter for President" yard signs. The four of us stapled to anything that wasn't moving over the course of two all-night undertakings.

The ruse apparently worked, and Carter beat Jackson handily in Washington County—something like 47 to 36 percent. We also won statewide, and Carter was well on his way to the nomination.

My work also seemed to impress Tim Kraft and others in the campaign because when it came time to staff the Democratic National Convention in New York City, I was asked to be the floor "whip" for the California delegation. In that capacity I had two Democratic legends, the late Frank Mankiewicz (Robert Kennedy's 1968 campaign press secretary) and the late Bob Moretti, (former speaker of the California Assembly) working "for" me.

It was a hoot!

At the end of the convention—actually on the Friday morning after the final session on Thursday night—I was interviewed by campaign manager Hamilton Jordan for a position in the fall campaign.

I'd heard and read a lot about Hamilton. I knew he had been the chief architect of Carter's remarkable climb to the nomination. He was young, smart, and refreshingly irreverent. But because we'd never met, and because I had no idea of what he knew about me, I went into the interview more than a bit anxious. A job on the fall campaign would be my real entrance into the political equivalent of the major leagues.

The interview went well. Hamilton said that I would work on the general election campaign, but he was unsure about which state I might be assigned or in what capacity. He said I'd likely go to California, but probably not as the state coordinator. Not too long after the convention I received word from Tim Kraft, by now the national field coordinator, that I would indeed be assigned to California in the number two position, under the direction of Terry O'Connell.

I went to Los Angeles a week or two before Terry's arrival and began to set up shop. After moving into the Carter headquarters (secured in during the primary on a very seedy block of Vine Street in Hollywood), one of my first decisions was to fire the woman who had been the headquarters coordinator in the spring. I do not recall her name, but it became quickly apparent to me that she was in way over her head and that she would be a constant pain in the rear if I kept her involved in any capacity.

My dismissal of this hapless soul led, in turn, to one of the more bizarre episodes in the campaign. Another staffer from the primary took great offense at my move, and he came bursting into a staff meeting one Sunday evening ranting and raving about my evil and contemptible character. He proclaimed that as long as I was associated with the campaign, Jimmy Carter had no chance of winning the election.

After trying unsuccessfully for several minutes to calm him down, I told the malcontent that if he didn't leave by the count of three, I was personally going to throw him out the (third floor) window. In considerably better shape than I am now, and outweighing and outsizing the guy by a fair amount, I thought I could do exactly what I threatened. The guy got the message, turned around and stormed out, still babbling about what an asshole I was. I figured that was the end of it.

Alas, I was wrong.

A week or so later, when I was elsewhere in the state, the guy returned to the headquarters, only this time he was brandishing a sizable butcher knife. He announced to the horrified office staff that he was going to get me one way or another. When told that I was not there, he took off, promising to be back.

Fortunately for me—but unfortunately for him—the guy's timing was bad. As it turned out, candidate Carter was due in town that week for a big fundraiser at the Century Plaza Hotel. When we met with the Secret Service agents as part of the advance preparations, we told them of our little problem with the guy and the butcher knife. We gave the agents his name and address, and never saw or heard from him again. We speculated later that they found and questioned him, and the guy either decided to make himself scarce, or he spent some time "resting" somewhere—courtesy of the Secret Service and the American taxpayers.

In addition to my responsibilities as the Carter/Mondale California field coordinator, I also had a special obligation to Norm Mineta: in 1976 he was going through his first reelection campaign. So, because I flew to Northern California at least weekly (sometimes more often than that), I frequently spent part of a day or so in San Jose looking in on and advising Norm and his campaign staff.

In fact, I spent Election Day and night in San Jose with Norm and his supporters at the San Jose Hyatt Hotel, where we celebrated his victory, and much later that night, the election of Jimmy Carter and Walter Mondale as president and vice president of the United States. The only sour note of the evening was that we failed—narrowly—to carry California.

I returned to Washington, D.C., a week or ten days or so after the election after putting in place a team and process to close the campaign apparatus. My intention was to resume my duties in Norm Mineta's office. I was not interested in a place in the presidential transition nor in the new Carter Administration.

My plan was to spend one or two more terms with Norm, and then to return to California, and *maybe* resurrect my own political ambitions. In the wake of the election, and after returning to the Hill, I wrote Norm an extensive and, as it turned out, fateful memo about how I thought the election results might play out in terms of presidential-congressional relations in general, but specifically how less senior House Democrats (those first elected in 1972, 1974, and 1976) could form the core of support for the new president. Like Carter, these junior House members tended to be more interested in results than in ideology, and they were, as a group, less reliant on the old, traditional Democratic base, and therefore less bound to old formulas, programs, and constituencies.

Unknown to me, Norm thought so much of my analysis that he shared it with Vice President-elect Mondale, who in turn gave it to his chief of staff, Richard Moe. Dick sent it on to Carter's Congressional Liaison chief, Frank Moore, with a note suggesting that maybe Frank should consider me for a spot in his shop. Frank apparently liked what he read, and he remembered me favorably from our brief interactions on the campaign trail. That led, in late February, to a call from Frank to Norm asking if he (Frank) could talk to me about a job. Norm said that of course he could talk to me, but he should know beforehand that "Les may not be interested in moving, based on what he's told me" (which was true).

Regardless, Frank invited me to meet with him in his office in the West Wing, which I was happy to do, never having set foot in that fabled portion of the Executive Mansion. Frank, Bob Russell, and I had a warm and wide-ranging conversation, which culminated in a job offer. I demurred initially, wanting to spend some time thinking about what such a move would mean to my career and to Norm.

I, quite literally, wrote down the "pluses and minuses" on a yellow legal pad. As I said later, "The minuses outnumbered the pluses, but the pluses weighed more." With Norm's blessing, I told Frank the answer was, indeed, "Yes!"

It turned out to be one of the best career decisions in my life.

The Giant Killer
Bill Fletcher

In November of 2006, the *New York Times* called Jerry McNerney a "giant killer." Anybody who knows Congressman Jerry McNerney knows how funny, even ridiculous, that really is.

Jerry McNerney is a soft-spoken West Point graduate and an engineer. An Associated Press reporter described him as "a little-known Democrat with a math PhD but no experience in elected office." Jerry earned his math PhD in New Mexico and settled in northern California where he worked primarily on projects related to wind energy.

Jerry presented as the furthest thing from a "giant killer" one could imagine. He was self-effacing, and the *Sacramento Bee* described him as "wonkish and facing a charisma deficit."

In 2004, his son encouraged him to run for Congress against Richard Pombo, then a powerful chairman of the House Resources Committee (now called the House Committee on Natural Resources) where environmental laws are written. McNerney ran a write-in campaign in the primary and won the nomination and then, predictably, got pounded by Pombo in the general election by a margin of 61 to 39 percent.

In 2006, McNerney decided to run again but the Democratic Congressional Campaign Committee (DCCC) backed another candidate instead of McNerney—a more liberal and wealthier donor who could fund his own campaign.

I had built my consulting business without the help of the DCCC. In fact, I often represented candidates like McNerney who had real connections to their district but weren't backed by the powers that be in Washington, D.C.

I was hired and guided McNerney to the Democratic nomination along with a talented team of consultants in defiance of the DCCC. Everybody thought McNerney would get hammered again because, in those days, congressional chairmen rarely lost their elections back home.

The first game changer came when powerful environmental groups across America decided to endorse McNerney, and suddenly, hundreds and then thousands of small contributions came in from all over the country. We were still being dramatically outspent by Pombo, who could raise vast amounts of money from political action committees in Washington, D.C., but we had enough to communicate our message.

The media strategy in our campaign, and in others, was dictated by the three media markets that touched the district: San Francisco, Sacramento, and Stockton. Broadcast television time in San Francisco was brutally expensive, more than $800 per gross rating point. Sacramento, by contrast, was just $212 per point, while Stockton was a cable-only market.

We decided to buy cable television only in the San Francisco market and put our broadcast media buys on the Sacramento stations. It was a decision driven by financial reality. We had enough money for cable television district wide but not for broadcast in San Francisco.

The money and endorsements from the environmental groups powered our campaign and, through the summer and early fall, our internal polling and some public polling showed the race between McNerney and Pombo had become a jump ball, with both candidates getting between forty and forty-six points, depending on the poll. It was, however, a given that Pombo's superior resources and the tendency of Republican voters to "go home" as the election drew near would probably result in a narrow Pombo victory.

Our campaign did finally get on the radar in Washington, D.C. The DCCC, thanks in no small part to the advocacy of pollster Celinda Lake, finally decided that McNerney had a chance. The Republicans responded by moving to protect Chairman Pombo. The airwaves were choked with advertising from both campaigns, both D.C.-based committees, and the environmental groups covering their bets. It was a free-for-all.

About a month from election day, I got a report from our media buyer analyzing all the election spending by committee. I noticed something peculiar. The media buyers for all of the different entities had made the same decision we had made initially ... cable television district wide, broadcast television out of Sacramento.

The San Francisco broadcast television market touched 39 percent of the district, but neither our campaign, our opponent, nor any of the committees advertising on the race were buying broadcast television in the City by the Bay.

I began to develop a plan to change our strategy. I spoke to our pollster (the wonderful Celinda Lake), our direct mail consultant, the campaign manager, and our field people because my plan would affect the entire campaign. Everybody signed off.

The plan we devised was to cut our spending dramatically across the board on everything that could be cut, and to preserve enough money to go up in San Francisco with less than a week to go. With all the different consultants and team members on the campaign agreeing to cuts in their programs, the campaign manager was able to identify just over $225,000 that could be made available. It was enough for a small but effective television buy, especially since we would have the San Francisco broadcast market all to ourselves.

On our next campaign conference call, the manager asked Jerry to attend to hear about a shift in strategy.

I presented the strategy to the team and the candidate. When I finished, there was silence on the line.

McNerney, uncharacteristically, exploded. He was furious. "You told me we couldn't afford San Francisco and now you're cutting everything to do nothing but San Francisco?"

Jerry's engineering brain just couldn't wrap itself around the concept of completely abandoning a previously agreed-upon blueprint for a wild, out-of-the-box shift in strategy.

Again, uncharacteristically, he rejected the plan and slammed down the phone.

Jerry wouldn't take my phone calls. I sent him an email with a quote from Ralph Waldo Emerson, "A foolish consistency is the hobgoblin of little minds, adored by little statesmen and philosophers and divines." I don't know if he ever read it.

I'm not sure how but, a few hours later, the campaign manager called and said, "Its approved. Do it."

Key to the plan was timing. If we went up too early, the D.C.-based committees and Pombo could easily scratch up a quarter million dollars and counter our San Francisco treat.

What most people outside politics and media buying don't know is how the timing of media buying works. At least in the campaign world, a campaign must have its media buy and money at the television stations by noon on Thursday to be on television for the weekend and early the next week. The media departments at local television stations won't change traffic or accept ads for the weekend on Friday. If you don't have your money there by Thursday at noon, your spots can't run until Tuesday or Wednesday of the following week.

I had made a television spot we were holding for the last week featuring wounded warriors from Afghanistan and Iraq looking into the camera and condemning Pombo for voting against money for better prosthetic arms and legs for veterans. At the end of the spot, the veterans said, "Richard Pombo added insult to injury." It was a simple, powerful, brutal spot.

Thursday morning before the election, representatives of the campaign walked into the broadcast television stations in San Francisco and presented the stunned advertising executives with a media buy, video tapes, and certified checks. We had not given them a heads-up because television salespeople are notorious for calling opposing campaigns to warn them about pending media buys from opponents to gin up more media buys and commissions for themselves.

Our spots began running on Friday. No other campaign bought broadcast television in San Francisco. The Pombo campaign and the Republican committee went bonkers.

They tried to sue us off television, sent threatening letters to the stations, and even tried to get their own television buys up on the stations on Friday afternoon to no avail. One of the lawyers even sent a cease and desist "order" to the stations that looked very much like a court order. All the stations just ignored it. Far be it for them to sacrifice their own commissions because of the rantings of lawyers.

Jerry McNerney was elected to the United States Congress from California's 11th Congressional District by a margin of 53 to 47 percent. Pombo was the only sitting congressional chairman to be defeated that cycle. McNerney's win was "the most significant electoral victory for the environmental movement in decades" according to the Defenders of Wildlife.

Having the courage to change a months-old strategy was key to the victory. But that's not the lesson I took away from that campaign.

A few months into his first term of office, Jerry McNerney fired me. He had someone on his staff call to tell me and wouldn't take my calls afterward. Efforts to reach him and talk to him were in vain.

A few months later, I happened to run into McNerney in one of the many tunnels under the capitol complex in Washington, D.C. He was aghast. If he could have melted into the concrete, he would have. We shook hands and spoke for a few moments.

I asked him what happened, and he told me that staff from the DCCC and the Speaker's Office told him if he wanted the DCCC's help, he had to hire one of their approved consultants.

"I just couldn't tell them no," Jerry said.

I reminded him that the DCCC had opposed his candidacy in the primary and he reminded me that the Speaker of the House was in his neighboring district. Case closed.

As I walked away, crestfallen, through the winding and meandering catacombs beneath the Capitol, it occurred to me, "Jerry McNerney had added insult to injury."

You Think Those White Folks Care?

Lincoln Mitchell

In 1997, I was managing the campaign for C. Virginia Fields, a city council-woman from Harlem who was seeking to become Manhattan Borough president. As with many races in New York City, the Democratic primary was the real campaign. Virginia was African American; the frontrunner was a progressive Jewish lesbian named Deborah Glick. There were several other candidates in the race, including Adam Clayton Powell III, who represented the district next to Virginia's in the City Council.

When I started the job, Virginia was trailing badly in the polls. But Virginia had some real strengths: strong backing from powerful political figures in Harlem, a solid centrist record on the City Council, and a bit of that star power that all successful politicians need. To win the race we needed to consolidate our African American support and compete with Glick in a white electorate that was liberal and heavily Jewish. It struck me as doable, but I didn't think it would be easy.

After my first day on the job, I spent the evening with Virginia as she addressed several different Democratic clubs around Manhattan. The first few stops were Midtown and the East Side. Virginia made an okay but not great impression on the voters there, but then we went to an uptown political club. At that club, which had a primarily African American membership, Virginia told an extraordinary story about growing up in Birmingham, Alabama. She described how, as a teenager, she had marched with Dr. Martin Luther King, Jr. and been arrested along with him and others. It was a moving and genuine personal story that showed Virginia's commitment to civil rights and to progressive causes.

As we were driving home from that event, I told Virginia how great I thought it had gone and urged her to tell that story wherever she went in Manhattan. She asked me "Do you think those white folks care about me getting arrested with Dr. King?" I told her absolutely they did. She agreed to start telling the story more and that we would use it in our campaign literature.

A few weeks before the September primary, one of Virginia's supporters told me "Virginia uses Dr. King's name so much, you'd think she was his running mate." I told him then that we must be doing something right.

Virginia won that primary by twelve points and served two terms as Manhattan Borough president.

Your Moses Was a Terrorist Too
Mark Siegel

In 1983, I got an unusual call in my office. The Reverend Jesse Jackson, who was reported to be considering a run for the presidency, wanted to meet with me. I asked Jackson's aide why he wanted to meet with me in particular. The aide said that Jackson "had trouble with the Jews and everyone knows that Siegel was the leader of the Jews on the DNC."

This was news to me but, in any case, I agreed to the meeting. However, I insisted that Thomas Dine, the new Executive Director of the American Israel Public Affairs Committee (AIPAC) as well as Sara Ehrman, an AIPAC lobbyist, to join us.

The day of the meeting Tom, Sara, and I waited at my Washington, D.C., office for Jackson to arrive. He was about thirty-five minutes late. We greeted him in the outer office, and then I invited him into my office. He walked directly into my office, sat down at my desk, put his feet (in cowboy boots) up on the desk. He said, with a big smile "give them an inch and they take a foot." He remained in that boots up position for the duration of the meeting, about half an hour long.

There was silence. I said that he had asked for the meeting and suggested we begin. He said that he was there because he wanted to have a truce with the Jews in the Democratic Party. A serious discussion began about comments he had made over the years, which were rightfully interpreted as anti-Semitic. He began explaining some of those statements, but then Sarah cut in, "Jesse, seriously, this is what you came to tell us?"

Jackson switched to the Middle East, expounding a reasonable, if left-wing anti-imperialist interpretation of the last forty years in Israel and Palestine. He talked about his friendship and respect for Yasir Arafat who he described as "a man of peace."

I interrupted, saying that from the point of view of Israel, and for most of the American Jewish community, Arafat was not considered a man of peace, but rather, as head of the Palestine Liberation Organization, a terrorist.

Jackson's face turned very intense, he looked me in the eye, and then made this remarkable statement, "Siegel, your Moses was a terrorist too."

Tom almost fell off his chair.

Sara rather hysterically blurted out, "Oh Jesus."

I told Jackson that before we talked about his charge that Moses was a terrorist, I wanted to know why a Christian reverend would say "your Moses" instead of just "Moses." I asked what on earth he meant by "your Moses."

Jackson then proceeded to ramble on about how Moses led an insurrection against dictatorship in Egypt and compared it to Arafat leading an insurrection against the Israeli occupation of Palestine.

I said, "So now you are comparing Moses and Arafat, that's your idea of a truce between you and the American Jewish community?"

The meeting may have lasted for another minute or two, but for Tom, Sara, and me, it ended with the Moses crack.

Jackson left, there was no rapprochement with the American Jewish community, which of course, is not a monolith and speaks with many voices. But it did have a very deep lasting effect on me. I swore to myself never to have anything to do with Jackson or any of his associates.

In 1989, my close friend and Kennedy associate Ron Brown was running for the chairmanship of the DNC. I would have been a natural ally, but Brown had run the

1984 Jackson for president campaign. Ted Kennedy called me into his hideaway office in the Capitol building and asked me for my vote for Brown for chairman. I sadly declined, again citing my problem with the Jackson connection.

Brown won. I resigned from the DNC. It was one of the biggest mistakes I have ever made in my life, one that I always regretted. But it always came back to "Moses was a terrorist too."

Perot Puzzle
William Sweeney

DeSoto Jordan was the head of the Washington, D.C., office of Electronic Data Systems (EDS)—Ross Perot's company—and was one of Perot's top lieutenants. He had been a contributor when I was at the Democratic National Committee and had become a client when I set up a consulting firm in 1985.

DeSoto called me up out of nowhere and said that Perot wanted to talk to Jesse Jackson.

I said, "Okay."

DeSoto said, "What do you mean 'Okay'?"

"Well, I know Jesse, and I know most of his lieutenants. It can probably be worked out."

"You're the only guy that I've talked to all day who thinks he has a way of talking to Jesse Jackson. Can you do it?'

"Well, let me try."

I knew that the Rainbow Coalition was meeting in Chicago. It was one way Jackson was sort of keeping his 1984 presidential campaign organization together for another campaign in 1988.

So, I called a friend who was one of Jesse's lieutenants. He was staying at a Chicago hotel, so I called the hotel and ask for him. The hotel operator put me through to his suite.

The call woke up a guy, and I asked if it was my friend. The guy said "no," and for a minute, I tried to figure out where my friend was.

Finally, the guy said, "This is Jesse Jackson. What the hell do you want?

"Well, Reverend, this is Bill Sweeney. You know me from the DNC days…"

"Oh yeah, yeah, yeah. Bill, what's on your mind?"

"There is this guy named Ross Perot, and he wants to talk to you. Have you ever heard of him?"

"No."

"He's a Texas billionaire. He is conservative, but he's done some stuff with education in Texas. He wants to talk to you."

"I've got this thing going on now, but here, this is my home number. I'll be home Wednesday and Thursday this week. He can call me then."

So, I called DeSoto and said, "I just talked to Jesse. This is his home number. He says he will be home Wednesday and Thursday night, and he'll accept a call from Perot."

"You're kidding?" said DeSoto, "I don't know how you did it."

"It's done. Okay, bye."

Well, a few months later, Jesse announces a trip to Europe. The thought was to develop his foreign policy credentials for the 1988 presidential campaign.

Fast-forward to the Iran Contra scandal in 1987. I'm sitting in my office watching Oliver North testify before Congress. He reported that he had the idea that Ross Perot should underwrite a trip to Europe by Jesse Jackson, so that Jackson could use his contacts with the Palestinian Liberation Organization to help obtain the release of a CIA Bureau Chief held hostage in Lebanon.

I called DeSoto.

"Are you watching Oliver North testify?" I asked.

He said, "No, I'm working."

"You better get a videotape of this fast. Why didn't you ever tell me that's what Perot was going to do when he called Jesse Jackson?"

"Because I never knew that's what Perot was going to do. Perot told me he wanted to talk to Jesse Jackson, and he never brought the subject up again."

So, from helping a donor, who became a client, whose boss wanted to talk to Jackson, to getting Jackson's phone number, to a phone call, to a European trip, to the Iran-Contra scandal—quite a puzzle. Perot did in fact underwrite the trip. In those days, Perot did a lot of stuff like that because he could do it—including his own presidential campaign in 1992.

Fast-forward another few years. I'm now working as the head of the Washington office of EDS, and Perot comes to a company reception in Washington, D.C.

Perot comes wandering in and talks with me and my wife. He knows of me but doesn't actually know me.

As we are chatting, my wife blurts out, "Well, go ahead and ask him."

I think, "Oh shit!"

Perot said, "Ask me what?"

So, I tell him this whole background about how I'm the guy that set up his phone call with Jesse Jackson.

Perot just looked at me and said, "My memory is not the same on that."

He walked away and didn't talk to me for the rest of the evening.

Right Ninety-Nine Times Out of a Hundred[*]
Jerry Austin

Jesse Jackson was a great resource in his 1988 presidential campaign because he knew where he wanted to go campaign and why.

One morning I was at campaign headquarters in Chicago—getting ready for the Super Tuesday primaries—when Jesse called at 5:30 am.

"I'm supposed to go to Tampa today," he said, "I don't want to go to Tampa."

"Where do you want to go?" I asked.

"Miami."

"Why?"

"I've been reading the papers this morning" (Jackson read three newspapers every morning: the local paper of wherever he was, *USA Today*, and the *New York Times*) "and the lead article in all the papers is that the government is claiming that the amount of drugs interdicted has gone down considerably in the last two years."

"I don't believe that's true," Jackson explained "I want to go to Miami, and I want to meet with the commandant of the Coast Guard to find out for myself if this is true."

---

[*] A version of this story appeared in Michael L. Gillette, ed., *Presidential Election Study Series: Snapshots of the 1988 Presidential Election. Vol. 3, The Jackson Campaign*. Austin, TX: Lyndon B. Johnson School of Public Affairs, University of Texas at Austin, 1992.

I knew what he was thinking already: great pictures. The guy thought in pictures—him standing next to a guy in a uniform, with a Coast Guard frigate as a backdrop, talking about drugs, with the pictures giving the message instant credibility.

In a matter of hours, we miraculously arranged for it to happen. Jesse went to Miami. He stood with the head of the Coast Guard. They went out on the frigate. When they returned, all the reporters were there.

Jackson said, "Commandant, tell the reporters what you told me."

The Commandant said: "The amount of drugs that has been interdicted has doubled in the last two years. The only thing that has been cut is the budget of the Coast Guard—by a million dollars."

Then Jesse said, "Ronald Reagan says, 'Just say no to drugs,' but he also says, 'Just say no' to the Coast Guard."

That was when the drug issue went boom in the campaign. Jackson became identified as the authority on illegal drugs in a way that set him apart from his competitors: a Black liberal who is very conservative on drugs.

Jackson had a good feel for this kind of opportunity. He was right ninety-nine times out of a hundred.

A Campaign Becomes a Crusade*

Jerry Austin

Jesse Jackson did very well in the 1988 presidential campaign. But after he lost the New York primary—and any realistic chance of winning the Democratic nomination—the campaign in the remaining contests became a crusade.

Then Jackson and I had a falling out.

I always knew we were going to have a falling out. In my mind it was never a question of if, it was only a question of when. A lot of people who knew both of us didn't give our relationship three months. We lasted a lot longer than that—almost all the way through the primary season. When we were good, we were very good. And when we were bad, we were very bad.

I was hired to be the professional to run the campaign. I was not hired to be "crusader rabbit," being involved in a movement beyond the presidential campaign. Unlike many of Jackson's people, I never was going to be with him after the election was over, whether that happened in April, June, after the convention, or November. I was never signing up forever.

---

* A version of this story appeared in Michael L. Gillette, ed. *Presidential Election Study Series: Snapshots of the 1988 Presidential Election. Vol. 3, The Jackson Campaign.* Austin, TX: Lyndon B. Johnson School of Public Affairs, University of Texas at Austin, 1992.

My training as a political professional was to cut your losses and see what you can get from what you have already accomplished. I felt that when you know you're not going to be the nominee, you say, "Let's go cut a deal with Dukakis. Let's be united. Let's have a part of this campaign in the general, if he wins; let's have a part in the administration." That's where my head was at. That's where I was going.

Jackson's head was in a different place. He thought it was not over yet, and he was going to continue campaigning. His training as a civil rights leader was that you never give up. Even though you may not be the nominee, there are other things to win. He would say, "We're winning every day." And in his mind, he was right. There were things that he was winning every day.

In his philosophy, the campaign was just a chapter in the history of a movement. The book wasn't closed. A chapter may have been closed, but another chapter opened. So, it was necessary to keep the movement going. He couldn't just say, "Sorry, guys. We're finished." Keeping the movement going, keeping people involved, getting delegates to make him stronger at the convention to fight for some issue planks—that's what motivated him. He wanted to "keep hope alive," as he said in his speech at the Democratic National Convention.

Jackson had loyal staffers who had signed up to be a part of his enterprise, whether it was PUSH or the Rainbow Coalition or whatever else he was involved with, plus he had the money to keep campaigning. But he would have stayed in the race even he had no staff or money. There would be people voting for him even though he wasn't going to be the nominee. That was building for the future, whatever the future might hold.

After the New York primary, I said some things I shouldn't have said.

When a reporter asked, "Do you think Jesse ought to be considered for vice president?" I said, "Of course. He's certainly earned that."

Jackson was infuriated. He said that I had no right to say that—that was something which, if he wanted it said, he would say. Jackson felt that saying that was like throwing in the towel. In his mind, if you finished a strong second, you were owed the first right of refusal of the vice presidential spot on the ticket. If he stayed the course, went the whole route, and it was mano a mano with Dukakis and if he didn't do anything to hurt Dukakis in the last month or six weeks, a vice presidential offer was something that he earned.

I told him, "There's no place in the Constitution or anyplace in the Democratic Party bylaws that states that because you come in second, you get offered the number two spot on the ticket."

Jackson said that I should not be a spokesperson for the campaign, that I should not talk to the press, that I should leave that up to him. He didn't understand that I was very valuable talking to the press throughout the campaign because I was able to do something that a campaign manager needs to do with the press corps.

I told him, "You need to have the press corps think of you as somebody who is not just putting out puff pieces and doing spins—that you can say, 'Yes, that was stupid,' or 'That was dumb.' It gives you some credibility with the press corps, which you need to have."

Later, when I was trying to get a feel from him of where he was headed, I asked Jesse, "Do you want Mike Dukakis to be president?"

He looked at me and said, "Why are you asking me that question?"

I said, "Well, maybe we get involved with Dukakis right now and cut a deal for the general and cut a deal for after that." Cutting a deal—not a negative thing. Just be involved.

"If Dukakis wins in 1988," I explained, "he's running again in 1992. If he doesn't win in 1988, you'll probably run in 1992."

He never answered my question.

Still later, I had a conversation with him in a hotel room in San Francisco during the final primary in California.

Jackson said to me, "I'm not going to be the nominee of this party because I'm Black. Democrats and white people aren't going to vote for somebody Black."

"Wait a second," I said. "Are there white people in this country who will never vote for anybody Black? Absolutely. But have you made a major dent in that? Of course, you have. Have there been white people voting for you in numbers that weren't there in 1984? Absolutely. "

"So, I don't believe that's why you're not going to be the nominee," I continued, "I believe you're not going to be the nominee because people are trained or brainwashed—depending on how you want to look at it—to vote for a vice president, a senator, a governor, once in a while a military leader—for president. People who have run something big and complicated."

Jackson said, "I'm a moral leader."

I said, "If we were electing moral leaders for president, Billy Graham would have been president a long time ago."

He came back and said, "Well, you're telling me that Lee Iacocca is more qualified to be president than I am?"

I said, "Jesse, absolutely, he's more qualified—in people's minds. He has run two major corporations. He's run something big and complicated. People aren't used to voting for a director of Operation PUSH or president of the National Rainbow Coalition to be the president of the United States."

After California, Jackson wound up saying what I had been saying after the New York primary.

Then there was this very hot rumor out of the *Boston Globe* that Dukakis was picking Al Gore for vice president. I called up a reporter that I knew on the paper and told him that I was infuriated that this would even be considered.

I said, "You can pick someone who didn't run, but if you're going to pick somebody who ran, you've got to give it to Jesse Jackson, or at least give him a chance to turn it down. If you don't do that, it's going to hurt you with the Black people in the fall. They're going to be offended that this man came within four hundred delegates of being the nominee, ran a terrific race, and you're not giving him at least the courtesy of turning it down."

Jackson went crazy about that comment, too.

I told him how all kinds of people from around the country were calling me, saying, "Jerry, you're right. I'm glad you did that. Somebody's got to show that the Jackson folks can't be taken for granted. We're pissed off."

There were some people in the Dukakis campaign who understood that they needed Jesse and a lot of Jesse's people for the general election. As it turned out, that didn't happen in 1988. But the Jackson's campaign did have a longer-term impact, including the election of David Dinkins, the first Black mayor of New York City, and eventually, the election of Barack Obama, the first Black president of the United States.

Race Was Not an Issue
David Yepsen

I think Jesse Jackson helped paved the way for Barack Obama in a lot of ways. That is not an original thought. Jackson took a lot of the novelty out of a Black candidate running—it just wasn't a big deal for a lot of activist Democrats. Obama was not the first Black guy to run for president. What they wanted to know instead was: Who is this guy Obama? Do we like him? In 2008, he was the perfect fit. New fresh face, good message, and some excitement.

Then Obama won Iowa and it immediately changed his prospects in the African American community in South Carolina. The common criticism of Iowa is that it is a 96 percent white state. But by winning Iowa, Obama showed he could win white votes. That impressed *Black* voters. Obama won the caucuses and carried the state in November 2008, came back four years later, and won it again in 2012. He had a good affection for Iowa and Iowans had a great affection for him.

Race was not an issue.

The Ditka Difference

Don Sweitzer

In the 1994 election cycle, I was the political director of the Democratic National Committee (DNC). One of my duties was to oversee and coordinate voter registration and Get Out the Vote (GOTV) efforts across the country. Reverend Jesse Jackson was a major—if not the major—advocate for an intense national voter registration campaign and a GOTV plan concentrating on minority communities in places like Chicago, Cleveland, and New York. Because I had a previous friendly relationship with Jackson, I was designated to work with him on getting resources from the DNC to the various entities working on voter registration.

Negotiating with Jesse Jackson was not easy. He was extremely demanding and relentless. His requests were usually well beyond the possible. The number of buses he was requesting us to supply for GOTV was far beyond our ability to underwrite. Oh, and he wanted us to supply him with a private jet to allow him to go around the country to coordinate and campaign for this effort. Our meetings and discussions on this issue began toward the end of 1993 and extended into the spring of 1994. We eventually supplied many, many buses—but nowhere near the amount he was asking for due to lack of funding. But we never gave him a plane.

I had known Jackson since the early 1980s. I met him during the presidential race of 1980 when I worked for Ted Kennedy, and got to know him better in 1984, when I ran the field operation in Cook County for Fritz Mondale. I had been to his homes in Chicago and Washington, D.C. A few times I went with him to the headquarters of his organization, the Rainbow Coalition, on the south side of Chicago, for one of his Saturday morning meetings—which lasted the better part of the day—and were a mixture of a religious service, a ward meeting, and a pep rally.

Early in our relationship Jackson remarked how much I looked like Mike Ditka, the legendary coach of the Chicago Bears. And, at that time, I did look like him. I was quite a bit heavier than I am now. I had a pretty good head of dirty blond hair and a bushy mustache, just like the coach. Jackson started calling me "Ditka," which he does to this day.

The resemblance to Ditka was not just something that Jackson noticed. Numerous times I was mistaken for him on airplanes and at hotels, particularly when I was in Chicago. One of my friends and I frequently had lunch or dinner with him at Ditka's restaurant when I was in town. We would always meet at the bar, which was nearly impossible the first few times because people kept coming up to me thinking I was Coach Ditka. My friend finally suggested that instead of getting into a long back and forth with these people on how I was not Ditka, I should just say "Hi thank you for coming in. Have a good time." That's exactly what I did, and the encounters became much shorter.

In spring of 1994, I was in New York City on my way back to Washington, D.C. I didn't have a lot of time to catch my plane, so I was running. Suddenly, I heard a very loud voice shout, "Ditka!" It was Jesse Jackson with the Reverend Al Sharpton, who I had never met. He was gesturing for me to come over to him. Even though I needed to catch my plane, it would have been a bad move for the lowly political director of the DNC to snub Jesse Jackson. So, I stopped running and went over.

I greeted him and told him I needed to get back to Washington, D.C. He said, "Fine this will only take a minute. What about my buses?"

We then engaged in a tense discussion that ended with him demanding that I get in touch with his people the next day with a final answer. Sharpton witnessed this conversation with a quizzical look on his face. Then Jackson said, "Ditka, do you know Reverend Al?" He then turned to Sharpton and said, "This is my friend Ditka." I shook Reverend Al's hand, and then politely asked Jackson if I could get on my plane.

Al Sharpton was running in the New York Democratic primary against U.S. senator Daniel Patrick Moynihan. The New York State Democratic convention was in Buffalo sometime in late summer. As a native New Yorker, I accompanied my boss, DNC chairman and later U.S. senator Paul Kirk, to the convention where he was to give a speech. Everyone involved—candidates and top staff—were backstage at the facility before the ceremonies started. As always at these kinds of gatherings, everyone was hanging out and schmoozing.

Sharpton approached me from the opposite end of the area. He stuck out his hand and said, "Mr. Ditka, we met with Jesse at the airport a while ago. I never knew you were an activist and so interested in registering people."

At which point I stopped him from going any further: while I would like to have kept the Ditka thing going, I could not. I gave him the history. We both had a good laugh. Sharpton went off, made a powerful speech, and then got creamed in the primary.

Rainbow PUSH Convention

Steve Rosenthal

In 1996, I was the political director at the AFL-CIO. I was in the job for two weeks when I get a call from somebody saying, "Steve, Reverend Jackson wants you to come to Chicago to speak to the Rainbow PUSH Convention."

I replied, "I'd like to come, but my mom is in the hospital in Florida. I really can't do it."

The response was "Reverend Jackson wants you to come."

I'm thinking, does he really know me? I had that encounter with him in Trenton. I've been on picket lines with him over the years.

Ten minutes later, I get a call from him.

"Rosenthal, it's Reverend Jackson. I really need you to come to this convention."

"My mother is in the hospital in Florida; I'm going down to see her."

"You'll come to Chicago, we'll get you on and off quickly, and then you'll go see your mother."

"Well, I don't even have anything to say. I'm new on the job."

"Well, you're going to be part of a discussion with a few other people. You don't have to prepare anything. You got to come."

How do I say no?

I go out to the convention. There's a choir singing. There's an organ and a band playing. They ushered me up to the stage. I'm on the stage now with Congressmen Dick Gephardt and Martin Frost plus several Chicago Alderman. There's ten or twelve people all on this panel. Nobody has any idea what they're doing there or what they're supposed to say or do.

Jackson asks a couple of people for some remarks and then he says, "And now Brother Rosenthal, the new political director at the AFL-CIO. He's going tell us how we're going take back the Congress this year." And he calls me up to the podium.

To this day, I have no idea what I said. I know that somewhere there's a tape of this Jewish guy from New York with the choir behind him and the band playing, speaking to the Rainbow PUSH Convention, and just probably blabbing about nothing for ten minutes.

Before the end of the session, Jackson passed the plate and said, "Now all of you up on the stage here, you're not exempt from this. Come on now Brother Rosenthal, take out that checkbook."

Now, I'm sitting there thinking to myself: I'm not seeing my mom; God knows what I said when I spoke; I probably made a fool of myself; and to top it all, I'm writing him a check.

Make a Plan
Steve Rosenthal

Do you know what the Analyst Institute is? It is a group of researchers, some from the campaign world, some from academia, and it has become the Good House-keeping seal of approval for testing tactics in the campaign industry. When progressive organizations, campaigns, or individuals are trying to learn best practices, they can hire the Analyst Institute to put together a scientific test of their ideas. They do lots of tests in elections and then they post the results. Interested people will then shop around campaign plans based on the test results from the Analyst Institute.

To me, it is like the old game of "telephone," where somebody whispers something in your ear, and it goes around and around and around, and it comes back at the end, where it's a completely different thing. Some of the error comes from misinterpreting the test results, and some of it is because results aren't valid for the elections in question. Some of it is good, but it's mostly, in my view, a lot of bullshit.

An example is the idea of "Make a Plan" Get-Out-the-Vote (GOTV) programs. Have you heard about this approach? There was a test done by the Analyst Institute that showed that when you ask to make a plan with people on how they are going to vote, it increases turnout.

Basically, they call you up on the phone or they knock on your door, and they say, "Mr. Austin, Tuesday is election day. Have you made a plan to vote?"

And you say, "Yeah, I'm definitely going to vote."

"Well, do you know what time of the day you're going to go? You going to go in the morning or the afternoon?"

"No, I usually go after work."

"Okay, and how are you going to get there? Are you going to drive or are you going to go some other way?"

"Yeah, I'll drive."

"Okay, well, thanks; we've got you marked down that you're voting on Tuesday..." And so forth.

During the 2016 campaign, I'd go into a state, and in the morning, sit down with the GOTV canvassers. It was almost like a focus group, where I asked them, "What do you hear? What do you see? What's the first thing they say to you at the doors?" Then in the afternoon, I'd go out and canvas myself because I learned a lot by doing it.

On the couple of weekends I was up in Philadelphia, I went over to the local Clinton campaign office, just as a volunteer. I walked in, picked up a GOTV packet, got the training from them. Then I went out and walked the precinct.

Well, here was what I noticed when I'd go down a block. First, the voter targets were much too narrow. You'd be walking up a street and they had these little post-it notes they would put on a door if nobody was home. You'd go to the doors on your walk list and there would be six or seven Post-it notes there because the Clinton campaign kept coming back and either the people weren't home, didn't live there anymore, or didn't want to be bothered. There would be several other Democratic houses on the street that weren't on the target list because for whatever reason, they didn't fit their GOTV targets.

Second, the whole "make a plan" thing was overdone. You would go up to houses, and there were handmade signs that said, "I made a plan. Please don't knock." Or "Baby asleep. We made a plan." They were basically saying, "We made a plan. Leave us alone." And people would open the door and say, "I made a plan." Literally, open the door, and say, "I made a plan. Okay, thank you," and close the door.

The results were very disappointing: in 2016, Clinton got 12,000 fewer votes in Philadelphia than Obama did in 2012, and lost Pennsylvania. It was extraordinary.

So, I went back after the election to look at the research that led to the "make a plan" approach. The Analyst Institute website said that a scientific experiment was done in 2008 in Pennsylvania primary. It found that when voters were asked if they "made a plan" to vote, it increased turnout four percent over those who weren't asked if they "make a plan."

The guy who did the research was at Harvard, and it took him two years to write up the results of the 2008 experiment because that's what happens in academia. Then around 2010, his report starts showing up in Democratic circles. In 2011, people were talking about it; in 2012, the Obama campaign starts to use it; in 2013 and 2014, it gradually seeped in and became a thing we were all doing. And by 2016, it's all we did.

To its credit, the Analyst Institute's research has a little asterisk that said, "Not enough research was done." The experiment was for one 2008 primary race in Pennsylvania.

But how relevant was this research to the 2016 presidential election? In the original research there were other GOTV messages being mixed in from other people, and then the "make a plan" approach helped to increase the turnout by a slight bit more than everybody else.

And now that everybody is just doing "make a plan," does it have an impact on turnout? This point gets back to practice versus science: people think that they know something which may not be relevant, and they don't have the experience to adjust to unexpected changes.

What do you do when the FBI director has said that your candidate may be a crook in the last days of the campaign? Should you be wearing blinders, only talking to a certain handful of voters, and asking all of them if they'd made a plan to vote? Maybe there's another discussion you want to be having with those voters at the door about why they need to vote.

Who is going to say, "We got to call an audible! We're at the line of scrimmage, and the defense has changed on us so, and our play won't work"?

We didn't have people with the skills, experience, and the gut instinct to say, "We've got to make a new plan!"

Swiftboating
Mark Siegel

Looking back, I often think about things that seemed so small at the time that ultimately changed the course of history. One of those game changers directly involved me in 2004. Many think it prevented John Kerry from being elected president. Let me explain.

Senator John Kerry was a multi-honored officer in the war in Vietnam, where he was awarded three purple hearts and the Bronze Star. He was the captain of a Navy Swift Boat that attacked the Vietcong along the many twisted rivers of the South. When he returned to the United States, he distinguished himself as a leader of the anti-war movement, famously appearing before the Senate Foreign Relations Committee and asking the chilling questions: "How do you ask a man to be the last man to die in Vietnam? How do you ask a man to be the last an to die for a mistake?"

One would think that Kerry's distinguished service to his country would be a major plus in his campaign for president, especially since he was running against George W. Bush, who avoided Vietnam by joining the Texas National Guard, and rarely showed up for meetings. But that's not the way it turned out in 2004.

In early June, seven weeks before the 2004 Democratic National Convention in Boston, I received a call from my friend, the journalist Robert Novak. Novak and I would frequently talk about politics and about the presidential campaign, and this conversation was another of his series of questions contrasting Kerry and Bush. Bush had low favorable ratings, and Kerry had quickly sewn up the Democratic primary season with his party united behind his candidacy. The polls showed a very close race.

Toward the end of a fifteen-minute conversation, Robert Novak asked me an interesting question. "What do you know about John Kerry's record in Vietnam?" I answered that I knew he had served in the Navy as an officer, had been injured, and honored with several awards—but not much else. And then I asked, "Bob, why are you asking me that? It doesn't seem to be an issue in this campaign."

Novak continued the probing, asking me if I had possibly heard any rumblings about people who served with Kerry and were now prepared to attack his war record. I said I heard nothing about that rumor, but I thought any references to Kerry's service to his country would backfire, highlighting a Democratic hero against a Republican draft dodger. I asked, "Why would the Republicans want to bring this up? It's one of Kerry's strongest points."

Novak said that Karl Rove was famous for an interesting political strategy, attacking an opponent's strong point and not his weak point. He then said, "I think that's what they are going to do." I asked him what he knew and then he candidly told me that his son Alexander worked for Regnery Publishing, a conservative publishing house. Alexander had told him that they were about to publish a book by John O'Neill who had taken over Kerry's command in Vietnam. He said that O'Neill was claiming that Kerry's war record was a fraud and told me the name of the book: *Unfit to Command.* Novak added that O'Neill had "hundreds of witnesses" to back him up.

I told my wife about the Novak conversation and we both agreed that I should contact our friend Robert Shrum, who was the Chief Strategist for the Kerry presidential campaign. I put in a call to Shrum, but it wasn't returned. I waited for several days and left another message. This time Shrum called me back.

I related in detail everything that Novak had told me about a campaign to discredit Kerry's war record. I mentioned the forthcoming publication of *Unfit to*

Command by O'Neill, Kerry's successor on the Swift Boat. I told him that Regnery was publishing it, and I wouldn't be surprised if it was being timed to cause maximum damage to the campaign.

Shrum sort of chuckled and said that Kerry's war record was the last thing they were worried about in the campaign, that any attack on his record would invite the Bush comparison and they would welcome it. I said, maybe so, that he was probably right, but wouldn't it make sense, now that we have a heads-up, to preempt the possible attack? Shrum said that would only give attention and credence to the story. He said, "Ignore it. We will ignore it. It's not a story."

On July 29, 2004, John Kerry accepted the Democratic nomination for president of the United States. Robert Shrum wrote his acceptance speech whose opening line was "I'm John Kerry, I'm reporting for duty." When I heard that I thought that possibly Shrum was going to try to knock the wind of the Novak story after all, but there was no mention of it. The polls were great. The party was united. Things looked good.

Two weeks later, on August 15, 2004, Regnery Publishing released *Unfit for Command.* Simultaneously, "Swift Boat Veterans for Truth" filed as a 527 issues committee, making it eligible for unlimited contributions and no federal reporting. Texas Billionaire Harold Simmons, a close friend a big campaign contributor to his friend George W. Bush, donated several million dollars to get the group off the ground and on the air. The brutal attacks on Kerry began.

O'Neill had assembled 250 Swift Boat veterans to sign a statement condemning Kerry's service. There were 3,500 sailors who served on Swift Boats during the Vietnam War. One of Kerry's crew on his boat, Stephen Gardner, signed the statement. All the other living members who served with Kerry actively supported his candidacy.

Almost immediately a barrage of seven brutal anti-Kerry ads began running with heavy media buys across the competitive states in the presidential election. The first were a group of wives of American airmen shot down over Vietnam. They claimed all their husbands had been tortured. But they claimed that they refused to confess to the war crimes that John Kerry accused them of, that he had given "aid and comfort to our enemies." The tag line was, "If we couldn't trust him then, why should we trust him now?"

Another ad quoted Kerry testifying before the Senate Foreign Relations Committee, accusing U.S. soldiers of rape, cutting off heads, cutting off limbs, desecrating bodies, and razing villages. "He gave our enemies what our husbands refused to give under torture. He betrayed us then, dishonored them, sold them out."

Another had three men who claimed to have served with Kerry. They accused him of lying about his record, lying about his purple hearts, lying about his Bronze Star, and claiming that his account of the battle was as different from truth as "night and day." "He was no war hero; he dishonored his country."

The Swift Boat Veterans for Truth ads followed the pattern of the Willie Horton ads that badly hurt Michael Dukakis in his 1988 race against George Herbert Walker Bush. And as was the case in the 1988 Willie Horton ads, the 2004 Bush campaign disclaimed any responsibility, saying that "unaffiliated groups put them on the air." Of course, they neglected to say that these "unaffiliated groups" were funded by the top contributors to the Bush campaign.

After eight days of the heavy media barrage, President George W. Bush called for the ads to be withdrawn—just as his father had done with the Willie Horton racist ads against Michael Dukakis in the 1988 campaign. The ads continued for a few more days and then stopped. They had accomplished their goal. They had changed the narrative of the campaign. Kerry's poll numbers began to plummet.

By November the race had once again narrowed, but poll data showed the attacks had badly damaged Kerry's approval ratings and evaluation of his honesty. On November 2, 2004, George W. Bush defeated John Kerry in the Electoral College by 286–251. If 59,300 voters in Ohio had switched from Bush to Kerry, Kerry would have won Ohio and been elected in the Electoral College by 271–266.

Can anyone believe that the Swift Boat media barrage against John Kerry switched at least Ohio against Kerry and elected Bush? I had given the campaign a heads-up about the book and the media ads six weeks before the book was even published. This campaign could easily have been deflected and marginalized in advance. But it wasn't.

John Kerry was "swiftboated," contributing a new verb to America's political lexicon. "Swiftboating" is now defined as "an ad hominem attack against a public figure, coordinated by an independent or pseudo-independent group, usually resulting in a benefit to an established political force. Specifically, this form of attack is controversial, easily repeatable, and difficult to verify or disprove because it is generally based on personal feelings or recollections."[*]

Another definition is even more to the point: "The act of discrediting a political opponent by making exaggerated or outrightly false claims about his/her character and past actions."[**]

---

[*] Dave Johnson, "The Swiftboaters Are Back in the Water," *Huff Post*, July 17, 2006, https://www.huffpost.com/entry/the-swiftboaters-are-back_b_25223.
[**] Viola Genger and Ryan Goodman, "The Swifboating of Joe Biden," *Just Security*, September 24, 2019, https://www.justsecurity.org/66290/the-swiftboating-of-joe-biden/.

III. Political People

The Best Retail Politician Ever

Ike McLeese

Strom Thurmond was the best retail politician I ever met.

Warren Abernathy, who was Thurmond's long-time administrative assistant, told me a story about when he and the senator were in Charlotte and driving to an event in Myrtle Beach. He had been able to get Strom on an earlier flight, so they were about three hours ahead of schedule.

They were driving on a two-lane road in the countryside, which was flatland with cotton and soybeans—very rural area. It was the middle of the week, maybe a Wednesday, and they came to this church with cars parked everywhere, just spilling out of the parking lot in every direction.

In the South, that can only mean one thing: a funeral.

Strom said, "Pull in here."

Warren said, "Sir, you don't know who it is."

"Well, they'll all know me" was Strom's response.

Strom enters this African American church and sits right in the front row with the family, tears running down his face, looking sad and concerned. He hugged everyone before he left.

I would be willing to bet that every single person at that funeral voted for Strom Thurmond for the rest of their lives.

On the Record with Strom Thurmond
Phil Noble

In 1978, I was doing opposition research on Senator Strom Thurmond for Charles "Pug" Ravenel, who was running against Thurmond for the U.S. Senate in South Carolina.

I was looking into Thurmond's votes in the U. S. Senate, when I saw that Thurmond had voted in favor of a fair housing provision of the 1968 Civil Rights bill.

"This can't be right," I thought. I did some more checking, and sure enough, that's what the congressional record showed.

Republican Senator Jacob Javits had introduced the bill, and I knew that Javits and Thurmond hated each other with a passion. There couldn't have been greater cultural dissonance: a liberal New York Jewish Republican, and a conservative South Carolina Baptist Dixiecrat. Both were on the Senate Judiciary Committee—they were just like oil in water.

"There's got to be a mistake," I thought. Strom Thurmond, one of the leading segregationist politicians in America, did not vote for a civil rights bill.

I called up a clerk with the Senate, and he pulled the original record, and said, "I've got the roll call tally sheet here in my hand, and Strom Thurmond did vote for the fair housing bill."

"There's got to be a story here," I said to myself.

I called Senator Javits's office. They didn't know anything about the vote, but the kind receptionist checked around and called me back and said, "There is a retired staff guy in New York who might know something. Here's his number."

I called the guy, explained who I was, and I said, "I have to ask you about a vote by Strom Thurmond for a fair housing bill in the 1968."

All of a sudden, the guy exploded in laughter.

Then he told me the story.

In turns out that in the Senate chamber, Javits sat in John C. Calhoun's old desk, and Strom Thurmond wanted that desk. In fact, the first day Thurmond arrived in the Senate in 1954, he asked Javits if he would trade with him for the desk. As fellow South Carolinians, Calhoun was Thurmond's hero. Traditionally, new senators carved their names in the drawer of the desk and Thurmond wanted Calhoun's desk worse than anything, so he could carve his name beside that of Calhoun.

When Thurmond first asked for the desk, Javits immediately told him "No." Thurmond became insistent, and an argument ensued on the Senate floor. That's when the animosity growing into real hatred between the two all began. Every few years, Thurmond would ask Javits for the desk, and the answer was always the same "NO."

Fast-forward to 1968. Javits had a landmark fair housing bill he wanted to attach to the Civil Rights Act that was coming to the floor of the Senate, and Javits needed one more vote.

He said to Thurmond, "I'll give you the desk, if you vote for the bill."

Strom said, "Let me think about it."

Thurmond then walked around the Senate floor for a while and came back to Javits just as the voting started. He said, "I'll do it."

Javits made Thurmond stand there beside him until he voted for the bill.

Immediately upon voting yea, Thurmond dragged the desk back across the Senate floor before the voting was even finished. He immediately sat down, opened the desk drawer, and began carving his name into John C. Calhoun's desk.

During the Ravenel campaign, we published a little campaign brochure based on my research on the record of J. Strom Thurmond, and we included his vote for the fair housing bill.

Late in the campaign, I just happened to be flying back from Washington, D.C., when low and behold, Senator Strom Thurmond came on the plane and sat right down beside me. The plane took off, but there was really, really, really bad weather, and they had to land the plane in Richmond, where we sat on the runway for at least two hours.

I had never met Thurmond. We started talking, and I asked him some questions about when he was governor of South Carolina. Then we talked about a lot of obscure things that happened in his early races. I knew what school he had taught in when he came back from the war, details of his 1948 run for president as a Dixiecrat—and lots of other details. He spent two hours telling me all this stuff—it was an amazing chronicle of a long life in politics. It never occurred to Thurmond to ask, "Why do you know all this stuff about me?"

After a while, he said, "I'm really tired, would you mind if I went to sleep?" I got him a blanket and a pillow and tucked him in. I just sat there looking at that old geezer sleeping; he reminded me of my grandfather.

I learned an important lesson that night sitting on the runway for hours. I detested Thurmond's politics, as he represented everything I opposed and ultimately spent the rest of my life in one way or another fighting against. But, on a human level, it was wonderful to just connect with this old guy and talk about some of the many stories and people of his long life in South Carolina and national politics.

As we were landing, I turned to him and asked, "Senator, could I have your autograph?" He said, "Of course."

I pulled out the campaign pamphlet I wrote detailing all the horrible things he had done in his long career in politics, "The Record of J. Strom Thurmond." I flipped it over to the blank back cover and gave it to him. He signed it "To my good friend, J. Strom Thurmond."

I still have that pamphlet. It is a wonderful memento of the campaign, but more importantly, it as a reminder about the importance of separating a person from their politics.

A Dick Tuck Moment

Bob Mulholland

Dick Tuck was a California political consultant and prankster who became legendary for making fun of Richard Nixon.

One time Nixon was campaigning across the state on a small plane. One of the advance guys gets on and sees Tuck sitting beside Nixon, talking to him as if he was a journalist. The advance guy throws him off the plane. The day continues, with two or three events, and ends up in Los Angeles that night for a big fundraiser. The advance guy walks Nixon up to the front of the dinner, and they stop for Nixon to talk to one of the tables. Suddenly, someone pulls Nixon's jacket from behind. It's Tuck sitting in the front VIP section. He says, "Hey, we need some more butter at this table!"

If anyone did that stuff today, they would be hauled off by security.

When Tuck was in college in the 1950s, Nixon was running for the U.S. Senate. A professor asked Tuck to advance a Nixon event. Tuck rented a large room, invited only a few people, and did a long, boring introduction. Then he asked Nixon to speak on the International Monetary Fund. Afterwards, Nixon said, "You've done your last advance!"

The classic prank was when Nixon was campaigning in San Francisco. Tuck had put up a big banner in Mandarin Chinese behind Nixon, telling the advance people it said, "Welcome to San Francisco." But it actually said, "Dick, what about the slush fund?" The slush fund scandal had just broken out in the campaign.

The other prank was when Nixon was on a whistle-stop campaign tour by train, speaking from the caboose. Tuck dressed up as a conductor and waved to the engineer to pull the train out while Nixon was still speaking. Caught by surprise, Nixon almost falls off the back of the caboose.

Then there is the time when Nixon is getting ready to speak in Fresno, California. Then the whole place goes dark. Tuck had shut off the electricity in a two-square block area around the event. There's no way for Nixon to give his speech.

That one doesn't beat the time at one of the Nixon/Kennedy debates in 1960. At the end of debate, the press has surrounded the candidates, asking questions. Then an elderly woman walks up and pushes her way through the reporters. She has a big Nixon button, as if she's a big supporter, and she says in front of all the reporters, "Don't worry, Mr. Nixon, you'll do better next time."

In 1968, Tuck made fun of Nixon's campaign slogan. He hired a very pregnant Black woman to walk around a campaign event in a tight T-shirt that said. "Nixon's the One!"

Tuck made fun of himself as well. In the 1960s, he ran for state senate in the Democratic primary. He called a news conference in a cemetery. He said, "I'm going to win this election with the help of these people." On election night, he is running behind, and said, "Just wait until the dead vote comes in." He lost the election and said, "Well, the people have spoken—the bastards."

Tuck was way ahead of everybody else.

I got close once.

In 2000, I'm in New Hampshire for the primary. I go to a George W. Bush event. Bush is speaking to about two hundred people, and his wife, Laura, is there.

Some university had passed out a survey with questions about candidate support. So, the event breaks up, and I pick up one of the surveys that was lying around. It asks, "Who are you going to vote for president?" And it had "McCain" written on it. So, a McCain supporter had come to listen to Bush and filled out the survey.

I take the survey and I go up to talk to Laura Bush. I say, "I want your autograph." I hand her the survey to sign, but I don't show her the McCain answer. She autographs it. Then I go over and talk to Bush. I say, "I want your autograph." He looks at the survey and I could tell he was confused. I later found out that Bush was dyslexic, a fact that never really came out in the campaign. I said, "Well, Laura's autographed it." He said, "Oh," and then he autographs it.

Of course, Bush lost the primary to McCain. I still have the survey with both Bushes' signatures, and at the bottom, "McCain" written for "Who are you going to vote for president?"

The River Bandits
David Heller

In 2016, lots of candidates were running for the Republican presidential nomination. I pulled a "Jerry Austin," something I've always wanted to do.

U.S. senator Rand Paul's campaign called because he was going to be in Davenport, Iowa campaigning, and wanted to know if the senator can take batting practice with the local minor league baseball team that I own, the River Bandits.

I said, "Of course! We'd love to have him."

The campaign asked, "Do we have to pay?"

"Oh no! Don't worry about it, it's our treat!"

Then I said, "You know what, I know all these people at the Chamber of Commerce who are having a forum with Paul."

The staffer aid, "Yeah, we're negotiating it now."

I said, "Why don't we meet at the ballpark? Great room, have everyone come in there, Paul can take his batting practice, and then do your forum."

The campaign said, "Great idea!"

So, I set it up. Paul not only wanted to take batting practice on the field, he wanted a full uniform and cleats. Of course, I gave it to him, so he would be in full uniform on the field. After batting practice, he would speak at the forum, and then do a live interview on CNN with Jake Tapper at the ballpark.

Then I take the guy throwing to him aside and ask, "Do me a favor and keep him on the field a little longer? Throw him a few extras. When he's ready to go, give him a few more, throw a few more pitches to him. Challenge him to hit something."

Sure enough, Paul was on the field a little long. Meanwhile, I locked the field house so Paul couldn't get back into the club house to change out of the uniform into his clothes. He had to go upstairs in his uniform and cleats. He did his full presentation, and he did the interview with Jake Tapper live—in a River Bandits uniform.

Talk about national exposure for the River Bandits!

The Real Fish Story

James Crounse

My first job in Washington, D.C., was working for Rahm Emanuel, who was the Political Director at the Democratic Congressional Campaign Committee (DCCC) in 1987 and 1988. I was in charge of the hot congressional races in the Northeast and Nebraska.

Rahm was a fantastic boss and simply the most effective, energetic, loyal person I've ever met. Of course, sometimes he threw sharp elbows and used strong language to get things done—that was his Chicago way.

One of our hot races was in my region. Congressman Jack Kemp, the former NFL quarterback for the Buffalo Bills and the congressman representing part of Buffalo and its suburbs, decided to run for the Republican presidential nomination.

Rahm thought we should go all out to win the open seat: it would be a huge statement win. He sent me up to Buffalo, and we recruited County Clerk Dave Swartz to be our candidate. Dave had been elected countywide a few times and was a very popular and capable politician.

Rahm wanted to put together a team of consultants he knew and trusted. For media, we got Swartz to hire David Axelrod, a close ally from Chicago with an excellent track record of producing great ads and winning tough races. We found an experienced and smart political hand to be the campaign manager. But before we had a chance to suggest a pollster, Alan Secrest pitched Swartz, and was hired based on his past experience in Western New York. None of us were happy about it, but we moved forward to win the race.

Rahm hyped the race within the Washington, D.C., community, and Swartz did a good job raising local money.

Money meant we could get on TV early. Axelrod and his team created compelling ads going after the Republican nominee, Bill Paxton. In those days, we needed a good poll a few weeks out from Election Day to help convince the big funders of Democratic campaigns to max out their contributions.

Secrest conducted a poll a few weeks out from Election Day, and the results were surprising and disappointing. We thought the campaign had great momentum, but the poll showed Swartz losing by quite a bit.

A few days after we got the results, I got a call from the campaign manager. He said he studied the crosstabs from the poll carefully and found several baffling numbers and inconsistencies. He thought the poll was flawed.

The campaign manager tried calling Secrest, who seemed to be ducking his calls. After a few days, he reached Secrest and pointed out the problems with the numbers. Secrest reran the crosstabs—and the results were even worse.

On Election night, we all convened at the DCCC to get results from all around the country. As the results came in, we saw that Swartz had lost, but were surprised that it was by a very narrow margin.

Secrest's poll, for whatever the reason, was not correct. We were all angry about it, because a good poll would have meant a huge boost in funds, and that could have helped us win the race.

The day after the election, several of us piled into Rahm's office to go over the results and dissect our cycle. We quickly started talking about the Buffalo race. Joe Sensheimer, a colleague, had a copy of an *Atlantic* magazine, and on one of the back pages, saw a display ad for a company that would send someone a dead fish.

Joe said, "Maybe we should send one to Secrest."

What started as a joke turned into an impulsive—perhaps immature—group project. Five of us (including Rahm, Joe, and me), chipped in $10 a piece, and we ordered a dead fish to be sent to Secrest with the message, "Thanks for all of your great work in Buffalo."

Weeks later, Rahm got a twenty-page handwritten letter from Secrest, blasting him for sending the fish, and airing out several other grievances he had. He said Rahm was filled with "hubris" and called him a "starfucker."

Rahm thought the letter was far more damaging to Secrest than himself, and he instructed us to spread it all over town—and that we did.

The tone of the letter was partially fueled by the fact that the dead fish was delivered when Secrest was on vacation. The fish sat on his desk for an extra week, one can only imagine how ripe it was when he opened the box.

The "Fish Feud" story was the talk of Democratic political circles in the beltway. Eventually it was a story in *The Washington Post*, a cover story for *Campaigns and Elections* magazine, and was featured in an episode of *The West Wing*, with the Rahm-like character Josh sending an enemy a dead fish.

The way the story is remembered is that Rahm sent a rival a dead fish. It's in almost every story about his background. It actually enhanced the view that Rahm was tough and took no prisoners.

But after all these years, as anyone in politics would guess, the rest of us are jealous that Rahm got all the credit. And that's the real "Fish Story."

Highest Compliments*
Jerry Austin

After running Jesse Jackson's 1988 presidential primary campaign, I had always thought I would have a role in the Dukakis general election campaign.

Eventually, I did get a call from the campaign in September from Chuck Campion, whom I knew. He said, "I want you to be involved. We need your help in Ohio."

To me that was a typical pattern of campaigns that Democratic candidates have run, where they only include their own, and rarely reach out to other people in a timely fashion. In the end, I did some TV spots to be played in Ohio and maybe other parts of the Midwest toward the end of the campaign.

I was pissed off by the Dukakis campaign.

I made some comments to *The Washington Post* right before the election. I paid the Republican campaign operatives—Lee Atwater, Roger Ailes, Craig Fuller, Bob Teeter, and Jim Baker—the highest compliment I could: if they had been running the Gary Hart campaign during the Donna Rice debacle, Gary Hart would be president-elect of the United States.

I'm sure that pissed off the Dukakis campaign as well.

---

* A version of this story appeared in Michael L. Gillette, ed. *Presidential Election Study Series: Snapshots of the 1988 Presidential Election. Vol. 3, The Jackson Campaign.* Austin, TX: Lyndon B. Johnson School of Public Affairs, University of Texas at Austin, 1992.

Interestingly enough, two or three days after the November election, I was sitting in my office, and the phone rang. On the machine it said, "Lee Atwater is on the phone."

I started laughing. I didn't know Atwater. A number of people have called me over the years, saying they were somebody else. So, I just figured that it was somebody else making a joke.

I picked up the phone and said, "If you're calling me because you need a Democrat in the cabinet, I accept, but I want the CIA."

The person on the line laughed and said, "Jerry, this is Lee Atwater."

I said, "To what do I owe this honor?"

He said, "I read what you had to say in *The Washington Post*, and I want you to know, that's the highest compliment I've ever been paid in my years in politics. I just wanted to call you and thank you for that. "

Then he said, "I want to tell you something else."

I said, "What's that?"

He said, "After our convention" (the Republican convention) "I sat down, and I thought about 'Who are the junkyard dogs out there? Who are the Democrats out there who really understand this business and who could give us problems?' You were number one on that list."

Atwater continued, "I knew Dukakis would never, ever involve you in that campaign. I just knew it. I knew that Dukakis and you wouldn't mix. The style of the people he has around him, the Boston/Harvard mentality. You're more blood-and-guts and streetwise and all that. I knew I wouldn't have to fight you. I want you to know that we think a lot of you over here."

I appreciated his call—a highest compliment in return.

Be Very Careful with Roger
John Zogby

In 2002, billionaire PayChex founder Tom Golisano announced that he would launch a third consecutive independent campaign for governor of New York. I received a call from Scott Reed, Senator Bob Dole's 1996 presidential campaign manager, who told me to expect a call from the notorious Roger Stone, because he and his team were looking for a pollster. But there was one caveat, according to Reed: "Be careful with Roger Stone." I assured Reed that Roger's reputation as a master of dirty tricks preceded him.

Roger's call came within an hour, and the polling budget was massive. Not only weekly tracking polls in the Spring and Summer, but also daily tracking by September, on-the-spot issues polls, focus groups, and tens of thousands of voter ID and GOTV phone calls. I found Roger to be charming, engaging, and respectful during much of the campaign.

On one of my trips to Albany, I paid a courtesy visit to the longtime state GOP chairman Bill Powers, who not only championed my work, but also raised a fortune from my public polling for the *New York Post* and other dailies throughout the state. I walked into his office and before even a hello, Bill said, "Be very careful with Roger."

A couple of weeks down the road, I went to Golisano's office in Rochester and met the tycoon. I asked if we could talk in an antechamber alone. I told him then that he should deal with me directly about polling numbers. I would always give it to him straight and unfiltered. In any event, the race for governor that year was a competitive one among the Republican incumbent George Pataki, the Democratic incumbent comptroller Carl McCall, and Golisano. At a few points, the three were bunched together in a statistical dead heat. As Election Day approached, Golisano's numbers started to slide, and then two weekends before the election, he disappeared. I continued to track and watched his polls go from 28 percent (in the bunch with Pataki and McCall) down to 21 percent.

That is when Stone called me and told me that I was going to have to turn those numbers around. He said that the candidate was thinking about dropping out, questioning his commitment about wasting a lot more money on another hopeless venture. I said that as of this moment, Golisano was dropping down to 19 percent. Stone said that I could not allow that to happen: to beef his numbers up and show him climbing again. I refused, saying that was not how I do things.

"Then he is going to drop out, and we will all be screwed," said Stone.

When I said no again, he told me he was going to talk to another pollster (a famous one whose name I won't mention). After a few days, I was pretty much frozen out of the remaining polling from then on. My last polling had Golisano at only 14 percent—which is what he got on Election Day. I heard that the new pollster had him within striking distance of winning.

The following Monday after the election, The *New York Post's* Fred Dicker wrote his regular column about how Golisano was purposely tricked by his pollsters to believe that he actually was going to win. It mentioned my name first!

The moral of the story: "Be careful with Roger Stone." Words to live by.

A Master of the Game
Ike McLeese

I never had the opportunity to get to know Bill Clinton, but I was told this story by a woman with the Democratic Leadership Council (DLC), which was founded in 1985 after Walter Mondale's landslide loss to Ronald Reagan. The goal of the organization was to steer the Democratic Party away from their "leftward" leanings toward more moderate to conservative positions.

People were telling her about this young governor of Arkansas by the name of Bill Clinton, who she should meet. So, she called the governor's office about a meeting, and Clinton said, "Sure come on out." She flew out to Arkansas, assigned with the task of spending a day with him just tracking his activities.

Shortly after she arrived, he said, "Let's go get lunch. You have the rest of the day and half of the day tomorrow to track me."

They go to this private club in Little Rock and after finishing lunch, he says, "Excuse me, but my friend George is over there having lunch, and I want to say hello."

Clinton goes over to the table, and she sort of trails behind to listen. As they're talking, George introduces Clinton to the other people at the table—three older, very well-dressed men.

Before leaving, Clinton turns to George and says, "Hey, I've got a problem with the state budget. You have any time this afternoon to come by and help me understand the finances?"

The acquaintance said, "Sure, Governor, how about four o'clock?"

Afterwards, she turns to Clinton with a skeptical look and says, "What was that about, Governor?"

He laughs and says, "Seems like you figured me out quickly. Those three guys are bankers from Dallas, and George is a local real estate developer. He's in over his head financially, and they're here to decide whether they refinance him or not. I figured that the governor asking him for financial advice would get him an additional three or four points on his evaluation sheet."

Bill Clinton is a master of the game.

Lessons for a Young Advance Person
Corey Busch

When I first worked in campaign advance in 1968, the title was "advance man." Times have changed, and along with the title today being non-gender specific, the role of today's advance person has changed as well.

I learned the craft of advance work under the careful tutelage of one of the nation's renowned and most respected political campaign managers and consultants of his time. Joe Cerrell operated out of Southern California and learned his craft while a student at the University of Southern California, alongside future political giants such as the legendary California Assembly Speaker Jesse Unruh. While in his twenties, Joe Cerrell endeared himself both professionally and personally to candidate and then president, John F. Kennedy. The roster of Cerrell clients over the years became a *Who's Who* of America's biggest political names...all Democrats.

In 1970, I was a senior at UCLA studying political science both on and off campus. After first meeting Cerrell during the Humphrey-Nixon presidential campaign in 1968, Joe was able to overcome his deep USC ties to hire a UCLA Bruin. I was assigned to do advance work for United States senators and other party luminaries who came to California to campaign for various state and local candidates.

I was given the opportunity to work with people like Hubert Humphrey, Birch Bayh, Frank Church, Mike Gravel, and many others. It was more than just a little heady for a college senior, but spending time with people who were dedicated to public service rather than merely to the accumulation of personal power ingrained an idealism in me that has lasted all my life—notwithstanding how strongly that idealism was tested during the Trump era.

Joe Cerrell was a friend of Frank Sinatra's attorney, Mickey Rudin, who would allow Joe to borrow Sinatra's private jet to move many of the out-of-state Democrats around California as they campaigned for local Democrats. By today's standards I suppose that Sinatra's jet would be unimpressive, but fifty years ago it was something to behold—especially for a twenty-year-old college student who grew up in a household where Sinatra music played constantly.

Ol' Blue Eyes kept his plane well stocked with snacks, booze, and tape after tape of his many albums—it seemed otherworldly to me.

On a campaign swing with Senator Birch Bayh aboard the Sinatra jet, I came to know what a wonderful man and political leader he was. I just can't help but pine for the time when people like Birch Bayh mostly populated the U.S. Senate. We talk today about bipartisanship as a form of nostalgia. To people like Birch Bayh, the issue wasn't about bipartisanship, it was simply about a legislative body where the members routinely put country above party, constituents above themselves, and who saw their colleagues as colleagues, not as enemies.

In 1964, Birch Bayh was flying in a private plane with newly elected U.S. senator Ted Kennedy. The plane crashed, and two people were killed. Bayh pulled a badly injured Kennedy from the wreckage.

As I flew with Bayh in Sinatra's small private plane in 1970, I couldn't help but wonder if the senator relived that horrific crash every time he climbed aboard a small plane. I was either too young to know better or just too brash, but I allowed my curiosity to get the better of me. I asked Senator Bayh how he felt about flying in private planes.

The senator told me, without hesitation, that he and his wife, who was also aboard the Kennedy plane, escaped without being seriously injured. He also told me that moments before the plane went down, Kennedy aide Edward Moss changed seats with his boss. Moss was killed, along with the plane's pilot.

It took a moment for that to sink in with me: the conversation revealed a man who understood the fleeting nature of life itself and the mandate we all have to carry on with purpose.

I learned an important lesson from that encounter with Senator Bayh: ask the question! The answer you receive may help educate you and may just tell you something about the character of the person you asked.

A Humbling Moment
Bob Ney

Every time there is an event in the U.S. Capitol Rotunda, there must be a House and Senate bill to authorize it. I carried the House bill to the floor to allow the Rotunda to be used when the Congressional Medal of Honor was given to Mother Teresa.

I got a nice call from the Speaker's office, and they said, "Come over and meet Mother Teresa."

So, I went over, and all the congressional leaders were there plus the Cardinal of the Catholic Church from Washington, D.C.

I walked in the holding room, and there in this overstuffed chair sat little Mother Teresa. It was like the chair was eating her—you know, she was a wee little thing. I was just amazed. I've met a lot of impressive people in my lifetime, but I was just amazed.

Newt Gingrich introduced me, "Mother Teresa, this is Congressman Bob Ney from Ohio, he carried the measure that allows us to use the Rotunda today."

She just nodded.

Then Speaker Gingrich goes through the logistics of the event with Mother Teresa: how we're going to go out there and all the press from around the world is going to present; President Clinton will talk; then other officials will talk; then the Congressional Medal of Honor will be presented to you; and you will say something.

Mother Teresa looks at Gingrich and everybody in the room, some of the most powerful people on earth.

She said, "I want to thank you for this honor. I really don't deserve it. But I will receive it. I will sell the medal and give the money to the poor."

Then she smiles.

There was awkward moment of silence—you could've heard a pin drop.

What are you going to say? "No, Mother Teresa, you may not…"

I had this vision of Mother Teresa saying, "Thank you so much. Do I hear a thousand dollars, do I hear two thousand?" and auctioning off the Medal of Honor to the highest bidder right there in the Rotunda with the whole world watching.

The Catholic Cardinal broke the silence.

He said, "Mother Teresa, we are going to write a check you can give to the poor, and we'll hold the medal for you in memory of this day."

It was a humbling moment.

A Rookie Mistake?

James Crounse

In 1988, my close friend Peter Hoagland was elected to Congress from the Second Congressional District of Nebraska, which is mostly our hometown—Omaha, Nebraska.

At the time, I was a regional political director at the Democratic Congressional Committee (DCCC), working for Rahm Emanuel. Peter's campaign was my responsibility, and I was thrilled he won a hard-fought and close race.

Peter asked me to be his chief of staff. I served in that role for his freshman year and helped him get reelected in 1990.

A few months after Peter was sworn in, he introduced his first bill in Congress. It was a bill to designate Nebraska's Niobrara River as "Wild and Scenic," a federal designation to prevent development along its shores.

It was a perfect first bill for Peter because he loved the outdoors, was an ardent environmentalist, and had taken several canoe trips down the river with family and friends.

However, the Niobrara River was not in our congressional district. There was opposition to designating the river "Wild and Scenic" by political leaders in western Nebraska, including Congresswoman Virginia Smith, a very conservative Republican member, who had represented the area for many years.

It was my job to rally our staff. Our legislative director worked hard to get the bill drafted. Our legislative aide did yeoman's work to prepare charts as well as helping prepare Peter for his maiden speech on the house floor to introduce the bill. And our communications director was ready to rock and roll with press releases and television interviews. I called Speaker Jim Wright's office to book podium time. We had it all perfectly choreographed.

On the appointed day, we set out to execute our plan.

Peter was set to speak on the House floor just before noon to formally introduce the bill. Our legislative aid John Minter accompanied Peter to the House chamber while the rest of us gathered around a television in Peter's office to watch.

As we watched, we were horrified to see Congresswoman Smith. She went to the podium and blasted our bill well before Peter was scheduled to speak.

My heart sunk. I thought I made a horrible rookie mistake. We had not shared our plan with anyone—perhaps someone on our staff had inadvertently mentioned something that got back to Smith, or someone in the Speaker's office accidentally told her. I didn't know how she was alerted. I should have checked on who was speaking.

But I did know the headlines in Nebraska would now be that Hoagland and Smith were in a fight about the Niobrara River, instead of what I had hoped for—that Congressman Hoagland had introduced his first legislative bill, had given a great speech, and was saving the treasured river.

A few more members of Congress spoke after Smith, and then it was Peter's turn.

It all went well. He did a fine job speaking. He explained the bill, referred to our charts, described how beautiful the river was, and how important it was that it be protected.

I felt awful and rushed across the street to find him and apologize.

When I found Peter, he was smiling and buoyant.

He put his arm on my shoulder and said, "Jim, it's all good. A few hours ago, I went to Smith's office, and I told her about the bill. Giving her a heads-up was the right thing to do."

If it was a rookie mistake on my part, it was also an example of what an honest and principled guy Peter was. He went on to serve three terms, serve on the Ways and Means Committee, pass important legislation, and receive a 100 percent rating from the Sierra Club and the League of Conservation Voters.

And the Niobrara River, all seventy-six miles of it, was designated by Congress as "Wild and Scenic" in 1991.

Possession is Nine-Tenths of the Law
Ike McLeese

I started out in politics working at the South Carolina legislature as a page, which gave me an opportunity to meet a lot of people in politics.

In the spring of 1965, U.S. senator Olin Johnston died in office. Shortly thereafter, Governor Donald Russell cut a deal with Lieutenant Governor Bob McNair: Russell would resign as governor so Lieutenant Governor McNair would move up to governor. And McNair, as governor, in return, would then appoint Russell to fill Olin's unexpired term in the Senate.

Former governor Ernest "Fritz" Hollings, who had lost to Olin in the 1962 Senate primary, decided to run against Russell to finish out the last two years of Olin's unexpired term in 1966.

The people who had worked for Hollings as governor didn't think he could win, and they had all moved on to comfortable jobs at law firms or other careers, so he hired a guy by the name of Crawford, who was running the state municipal association, to be his campaign manager. Crawford then hired a guy who was an on-air broadcaster to be press secretary—and that was all the staff Hollings had.

So, Crawford put the word out at the university to recruit bright young men for the campaign. The people who were doing the recruiting approached me to see if I wanted to join the campaign. I said, "Yes." They also brought in Joe Riley, who became the "lifetime" mayor of Charleston, and Doug Dent, who became a politically active lawyer in Greenville. Riley was in law school at the time, and the rest of us were undergrads. As soon as the campaign got underway, it got out that we were the Hollings "campaign task force." We were labeled the "Diaper Brigade" by some of the news writers.

We then went after Olin Johnston's former staff because they thought Russell should have appointed Olin's widow, Gladys Johnston, to fill his unexpired term rather than cutting a deal to get the appointment himself. As a result, they put their weight behind Hollings.

We ended up beating Russell in the Democratic Primary in the spring of 1966. In the fall general election, we faced a Republican, Marshall Parker. We ran a minimal campaign effort because we did not take Parker seriously. But times were changing in South Carolina—after all, Strom Thurmond had switched to the Republican Party in 1964.

Hollings lost the upstate vote to Parker and almost lost the election. At around two o'clock in the morning, Hollings was only up by a few hundred votes. The next morning, when all the votes were counted, Fritz had received almost every African American vote in the state, but we were ahead by just a few thousand votes.

Then Hollings got a call from Vice President Hubert Humphrey, who said, "I see that you're still leading."

Hollings said, "Yeah, but it's really close. They're calling for a recount. I don't know what's going to happen."

Humphrey asked, "Your secretary of state, is he a Democrat?"

"Yes sir, he is."

"Would he certify you as elected?"

"I think he would. We are leading."

"Get him to sign the papers." Humphrey advised.

"Then get a charter plane and get yourself to Washington, D.C. I will meet you at the Capitol, and we'll swear you in. Possession is nine-tenths of the law."

Hollings ended up winning by a small margin, but that is how he got into the U.S. Senate in 1966, gaining seniority over other senators elected that year. As an incumbent, he handily beat Parker in a rematch in 1968 for a full six-year team.

The rest of his career is history.

What Might Have Been
Mark Siegel

One of the very special things about being an American Political Science Association Congressional Fellow to Senator Hubert Humphrey were those private, after-hours talks in his office, one on one. Humphrey took his mentoring responsibilities quite seriously. He would always call me into the office after six o'clock when the work of the Senate was usually finished for the day. He would be relaxed. Sometimes he had a drink. And he would begin each of these talks by asking a question: "Mark, what did you learn today?" Knowing that I would be confronted with this question at the end of the day was very much on my mind all through the day. I kept thinking all day what I would say that night.

Once, something very productive came out of this drill. I had read that in a Baltimore house fire three children died because their pajamas ignited. I checked with Betty Furness, who was the Democratic grand dame of consumer protection, and she confirmed while the Flammable Fabrics Act was adopted in the 1950s, it didn't specifically target children's bedclothes. She suggested that an amendment could be drafted to the Consumer Protection Act pending before Congress that would address this issue.

So that night when Senator Humphrey asked me the inevitable question, I was ready with an answer. I told him about the fire and about my conversation with Betty

Furness. I told him that additives could make flammable cloth nonflammable, and if put in children's sleep clothes, probably could save lives. He lit up, asked me if I was sure, and then grabbed the phone and called his best friend in the Senate, Bob Dole.

I would always tell this story to my students when I taught at George Washington University and American University for a couple of reasons. First, it was extraordinary that liberal Humphrey's best friend was a conservative Republican, Bob Dole. They were friends, their wives and children were friends, and these two men always looked for areas where they could work together. The Food for Peace program was one of the most important products of their friendship and collaboration. That kind of relationship is very rare in the Congresses of the new millennium. Second, the amendment was tacked onto legislation with bipartisan support without anyone asking if it would help the Democrats or help the Republicans. What counted then, and I sadly say not now, is that it would help save children's lives.

One night, after work when I was called into office, I was the one who asked a question. I asked him what he thought would have happened if Robert Kennedy had not been assassinated in 1968. Did he think he or Kennedy would have gotten the Democratic presidential nomination? I remember his answer very clearly: he smiled and said, "both." And then he explained.

He said that since I was an expert on delegate selection, I knew how delegates to the 1968 Democratic National Convention were selected. Most of these processes were closed. Primaries were few and often nonbinding. In many states, party leaders, and often-incumbent Democratic governors, handpicked their states delegates to the Democratic National Convention. That would change in 1972, but it still very much was the norm in 1968.

Humphrey told me that he and Bobby were friends and called Kennedy a "class act." He recalled that during the West Virginia primary, the Humphrey campaign had basically bought the support of key county officials with campaign contributions, who then promised to deliver the county to Humphrey. But on election night, the county went strongly for Kennedy. A week later Bobby reimbursed him for the amount he had spent—with a note that said something about being "outbid." Humphrey smiled. He said again, "class act."

Humphrey said very few people knew that during the campaign, he and Bobby occasionally talked, even well before Kennedy entered the race. He told me that he liked Bobby, and he was sure that Bobby liked him. He said that Johnson never knew about that, "Thank God." And then Humphrey said something that was quite extraordinary. He said that he thought he and Bobby had an accommodation, an understanding. He said that Bobby fully expected to win the nomination. He said Kennedy was confident he would sweep the California primary and a week later the New York primary, and then many of the uncommitted blocs of delegates that Humphrey was counting on would switch to Kennedy. Humphrey specifically remembered that Bobby had said that "Daley and the entire Illinois delegation" would be the first to switch. But then Kennedy added, "If it's not me, it must be you, Hubert. Gene McCarthy doesn't have the temperament to be the president."

Humphrey said that he told Bobby that there was a very solid count of delegates and that LBJ would never allow Kennedy to get the nomination, and that the president had continuing control of many of the governors and delegations. Humphrey was sure he was going to get the nomination, but the convention could very well be horribly divisive and the party badly split. Humphrey then told Kennedy that the stakes for the country were too high to allow that to happen. He said Bobby agreed.

Humphrey then told me that he offered Robert Kennedy the vice presidency. I think he told me what he actually said: "Bobby, I know you say you're going to win, but let's talk about if you don't win. If I am nominated, I want you to be my vice president. For me, for the party, for the country."

He told me that Kennedy did not make a commitment, but he seemed open to at least thinking about it. Bobby also thought the convention was going to be very divisive and could split the party in two. He said, "We can't let that happen." Indeed,

Bobby tacked on a contingency that would make it more likely that the Democratic National Convention adopt a Vietnam War "Peace Plank" as part of the party platform. They both agreed that Johnson would be furious, but it would transform the convention into a huge political celebration of accommodation and unity. The ticket would be powerful and would likely defeat Nixon. Bobby also said something about Humphrey agreeing to serve only one term, or at least that is what Humphrey remembered.

I was a bit skeptical. What I thought but did not say to Senator Humphrey was if LBJ controlled enough delegates to nominate Humphrey, didn't he control enough to stop a peace plank from being adopted?

Many years later I served on the National Democratic Institute Board with Ted Sorenson. At one point Sorenson appeared before my class at the George Washington University's Graduate School of Political Management, where I was teaching a course in speechwriting and speech presentation. The class viewed John F. Kennedy's famous speeches, and Ted Sorenson lectured them on how these critical speeches were prepared. It was a great class.

After the class, Sorenson and I went out to dinner. Both Bobby Kennedy and Hubert Humphrey were long dead. Thirty years had passed. So, I just told Ted Sorenson, who was close to Kennedy, what Hubert Humphrey had told me in early 1972. At first Sorenson said he wasn't aware of that and that he was much closer to JFK than RFK. But then he said he heard some talk about Humphrey and Kennedy uniting behind a Vietnam War peace plank, so maybe there was more to the vice presidential discussion than he had ever known. "After all, Bobby wanted to be Lyndon Johnson's vice president, although I can't imagine that those two would agree on anything." And then he said that possibly he did remember the vice presidency discussed in the context of Humphrey running for a single term.

I would later become a close friend of Ted Kennedy. Not only were we politically, professionally, and personally close, but we were also neighbors in Kalorama, a tony section of Washington, D.C., between Georgetown, Dupont Circle, and Adams Morgan. We would meet in the neighborhood dog park with our respective dogs, Splash and Willie.

I told Ted about my conversations with Humphrey. He did confirm (with a laugh) the payment by Bobby to Humphrey to reimburse for outbidding him in the West Virginia 1960 presidential primary. He also confirmed that Bobby liked Humphrey and really disliked McCarthy. He said there was discussion of the vice presidency—brief, casual, and highly speculative. But both he and his brother thought Bobby would have been nominated and elected.

The point is that a Humphrey-Kennedy ticket tied to a Vietnam War peace plank would have almost certainly united the party, and the Chicago Convention would not have been a debacle. Humphrey would have been elected president.

President Hubert Humphrey. Vice President Robert Kennedy. And then President Robert Kennedy. No Nixon. No Watergate. The War in Vietnam ending five years earlier with tens of thousands of lives saved.

We will never know what would have happened because Bobby Kennedy took a shortcut through a hotel kitchen after his California triumph. We will never know, but in the words of the ending of Ernest Hemingway's *The Sun Also Rises*, "Isn't it pretty to think so?"

What I Say and What I Do
Mark Weaver

Early in my career in Pennsylvania, I was helping candidates with the press. One candidate was fighting a battle against the local telephone company because, back then, you could call a "976 sex line," get someone to talk dirty to you, and it would be charged to your phone bill. They were like X-rated movies on the phone. This was pre-internet.

The candidate had gotten a lot of traction in the media for advocating that the phone company end this service. I got him booked live on a Philadelphia television program, in what was then the fourth-largest market in the country. It was going to be one of the midmorning shows.

I prepped him with the talking points. He was going to debate a representative of the phone company. We rehearsed during the drive to the TV station. He was quiet during the last fifteen minutes of the drive.

I thought, "He's getting in the zone for this live television debate!"

We were parking the car when he said, "Do you think the phone company has access to people's records and numbers who called those 976 lines?

I said, "Is there something you want to tell me?"

"Well, those sex lines? I've been calling them lately. This fellow from the phone company might know that, so what should I do if he brings it up?"

I said, "My best advice is to say it is a violation of privacy and professionalism for him to look at an individual's phone bill."

Fortunately for the candidate, the topic never came up. But it is another example of a politician quick to say one thing and then do another.

Trust but Verify

Jerry Austin

In 1994, I was doing a race for the governor of Oklahoma. My candidate was a state senator who was the first woman running for governor. Her primary opponent was the lieutenant governor. The way it worked in Oklahoma at the time was that if no candidate got fifty percent in the primary, a runoff took place three weeks later.

We were way behind, and I said to my candidate, "You know a woman running for governor, people are going to think you're soft on crime."

She said, "I'm not soft on crime. I'm a champion for the Judiciary Committee, and I'm the author of the capital punishment bill. Besides that, I'm a victim of crime."

I said, "Really, what happened?"

She said, "I was in my hometown and was walking down the street, when a guy came and ripped my handbag out of my arm. I kicked off my shoes, and I went after him. I didn't catch him, but I was able to pick him out of a lineup and he's in jail."

I recreated the story in slow motion: snatching of the bag, shoes off, and running after the thief. It ended with the candidate looking up at the camera and saying, "Some people think as a woman is soft on crime. Not this woman."

I put the spot on the air, and we suddenly went from 3 to 43 percent. We held the lieutenant governor to under fifty percent of the vote. We were going into the runoff in three weeks.

Three or four days later, the political reporter for the *Tulsa World* wrote a story about the spot that catapulted my candidate from nowhere to somewhere. It turned out that the candidate made the whole thing up. She lied. There was no robbery or report of a robbery, and there was nobody that she identified in a police lineup. All the reporter did was go to the hometown police station and found out that it wasn't true. When the reporter asked the candidate why she lied, her response was, "I guess I've been telling that story so many years that I believed it was true."

I learned a lesson: trust but verify what your candidates tell you.

Fighting Fritz

Joe Trippi

One of my prize possessions is a red boxing glove, one of a pair given to me by the late vice president Walter "Fritz" Mondale. The story of these gloves will tell you the kind of man Fritz was and why he means so much to me.

In December 1983, I was in my twenties and running the Iowa presidential campaign for Fritz. At the end of every campaign swing through Iowa, after loading the campaign plane with traveling staff and a huge press corps assigned to the campaign, Fritz would come down the steps of the plane and take me on a stroll two or three times around the aircraft.

The conversation always ended the same way: Fritz telling me that he could not lose Iowa and that he was counting on "The Hogs" (what the Mondale Iowa campaign staff proudly called ourselves) to do everything we could to make sure he won the first-in-the-nation caucuses.

"Don't let up. Keep fighting," he would say—and then back on the plane he went and off to another campaign stop.

During these strolls, we also talked about all kinds of things before we got to the "no pressure, just don't blow it" end of the talk.

One day we were talking about my family, when Fritz asked about my father—a question I dreaded.

I explained that my father had stopped talking to me five years earlier, when I left college to join Ted Kennedy's 1979 presidential campaign against Jimmy Carter and Walter Mondale.

My dad was old school Italian. I was supposed to take over his flower shop, not go to college, and then, of all things, to run off before graduating and become a political hack.

Fritz joked with me that my dad was wrong about a lot of things, but maybe I should have listened to him about going to work for Kennedy.

I was one of only a handful of Kennedy operatives hired in the Mondale campaign. I was lucky to have worked for both Ted and Fritz. But at the time, there was still a lot of bad blood. Fritz was joking, but still I was relieved when he got to the "we must win Iowa" ending of the talk.

About a month later, we won Iowa with 49 percent of the vote, with Gary Hart taking a distant second. But that was enough to get Hart into the media spotlight and give him the momentum he needed to win New Hampshire.

The Hart campaign took off like a rocket, and the campaign became a struggle.

Over the next set of primaries, "Fighting Fritz" emerged as the narrative of our campaign.

Mondale would walk on to the stage at rally after rally, thrust a pair of red boxing gloves in the air and speak from the heart about who he was fighting for.

I remember traveling with him to a meatpacking plant, and Fritz bellowing, "Show me your hands!"

My jaw dropped as worker after worker thrust a hand in the air with fingers missing that they had lost on the job. I had no idea—but Fritz did.

It was those people Fritz was fighting for.

Soon time and delegates were running out on us, and the delegate-rich Pennsylvania primary was crucial to our cause. It was held in April—months after we won Iowa.

I was sent in as state director of Pennsylvania in March, and we were down by fourteen points. I had nightmares about losing Iowa, but they were nowhere near as bad as the ones I had about losing Pennsylvania.

Fritz and I resumed the tarmac strolls as he campaigned across the state.

No pressure, Joe, but "Fighting Fritz" needs you and all the staff to not let up, remember who we are fighting for.

Fritz won Pennsylvania. It was a comeback win among comeback wins.

After the networks called Pennsylvania for Fritz, I was summoned up to the candidate's hotel suite. When I walked through the door, there was the former vice-president explaining to an old Italian guy, "Your son is in an honorable profession, fighting for people who are down and hurting. He's making a difference. I count on him, and you need to know that."

Fritz remembered what I had told him months ago—eons in the life of a presidential campaign. He had somehow located my dad and got him to Philadelphia on primary night.

As my father hugged me, the aide broke the spell.

He said, "Sir, we have to get downstairs for your speech," handing Fritz his fighting gloves.

"I don't need these anymore," Fritz said.

He took a felt tip pen and wrote on the gloves, "To Rocky Trippi with thanks, Fritz Mondale." It was from the movie *Rocky*, where the title character, an Italian boxer from Philadelphia, has an incredible comeback.

Fritz gave his fighting gloves to me.

Then Fritz took my dad with him to the ballroom and dragged him on stage to stand with him as he gave his victory speech.

I still tear up thinking about that moment in my life.

Years later, when my father passed away, I gently tucked one of the gloves into his casket.

RIP Fritz.

Protocol vs. Passion
William Sweeney

Congressman Jim Corman regularly connected people and opportunities to help the Democratic Congressional Campaign Committee (DCCC). In early 1977, Vice President Walter Mondale pledged to visit Los Angeles on behalf of the DCCC. Jim shared Mondale's pledge with Lew Wasserman, who was arranging a John Denver concert at Universal Studio amphitheater. I was assigned to organize the fundraising event.

John Denver donated his services. He had one request: Would Vice President Mondale introduce him?

I had worked with the Mondale team since 1974 and informed them of Denver's request. Since I had already scripted assorted Democratic events, this ask did not seem to be a big deal to me.

I was surprised when I was universally and emphatically turned down by everybody in the Mondale office: "THE VICE PRESIDENT OF THE UNITED STATES does NOT introduce entertainment!"

My real problem became that John Denver really wanted to be introduced by Mondale—as his agent repeatedly informed me.

I finally went to Corman and detailed all my conversations at the staff level. Jim laughed and said, "No problem."

Later that week, Corman attended a White House meeting, had a conversation with Mondale, and brought up Denver's request. Mondale says he'd be thrilled. Denver was one of his favorite artists; he had done so much for the environmental movement and other causes; and now was doing this concert for the DCCC.

Mondale was delighted with the opportunity.

I was in the doghouse with the vice president's staff for a while.

But on a beautiful June evening, Walter Mondale gave a warm introduction of John Denver from his heart.

Dick Cheney and the Bicycle Wheel
Mark Siegel

The American Political Science Association selected me as a Congressional Fellow for the 1971–1972 class. I was a PhD candidate in political science from Northwestern University and received my doctorate in June of 1972. Two years before, Richard Cheney was a Congressional Fellow in the 1968–1969 class. He was a PhD candidate in political science from the University of Wisconsin in Madison. He never finished his degree.

Our lives intersected first as part of the Congressional Fellow program, and then, partly because of the Congressional Fellowship relationship, in the White House during the Carter transition after the 1976 presidential election.

There are two traditional management models for presidential leadership in the White House. The "hierarchical pyramid" model, with the president on top and a strong chief of staff immediately below, is based on the military chain of command. The chief of staff is the most powerful position in the model, commanding huge authority and all access and information to the president. This model relieves the president from the cumbersome burden of running the White House, freeing him to make broad leadership decisions. It is a classic example of centralization of power and authority.

A competing presidential management model is often referred to as "the spokes of the wheel" model. In this model, the president is the dominant manager of the

White House. He runs the shop. The chief of staff, if there is one, has dramatically diminished power. All assistants to the president have equal access to the president. This model demands that the president have strong leadership style and a great command for detail. It is a classic example of the decentralization of power. Its major disadvantage is that details and staff management burden the president, who can become consumed by detail, losing focus on broader leadership decisions.

President Eisenhower, a former general of the army, was most comfortable with the pyramid hierarchical military model with a powerful chief of staff controlling all access and information to him. President Reagan adopted the same management style as Eisenhower. President Roosevelt embraced a modified position, where he had a chief of staff but encouraged staff access and competing ideas from his staff. President Lyndon Johnson was an adherent of the spokes of the wheel model until he became immersed in the day-to-day management of the war in Vietnam, when he switched to the pyramid hierarchical model.

When Jimmy Carter was elected president, I was assigned a position in transition on cabinet selection. The president-elect strongly believed that the Watergate scandal of the Nixon administration was encouraged by a strong chief of staff who cut off information access to the president. In the early days of the transition, President-elect Carter made it clear that he would adopt an extreme version of the spokes of the wheel model, with no chief of staff. Although his campaign manager Hamilton Jordan was believed to be the most powerful staffer, he officially had the title of assistant to the president along with eight other White House staffers. Under the model, and in practice, each assistant to the president had equal access to the president, and each controlled the information in his portfolio of responsibility that landed on the president's desk. It was exactly like a bicycle wheel, with the president in the center and equal spokes emanating from and to the center. There had been no president in the twentieth century without a chief of staff—Jimmy Carter was to be the first.

Because of my relationship with Dick Cheney, the chief of staff in Gerald Ford's White House, the transition designated me as his liaison. The Ford-Carter election had been heavily contested and quite close in the end, but it was a civil and clean campaign that never generated personal enmity between the two candidates. Because of that, and stemming from my past relationship to Cheney, our working relationship was smooth and professional. After the November election, I would meet from time to time with him in the chief of staff's rather imposing office close to the Oval Office.

In late December, I told Cheney about Carter's view about the hierarchical model under Nixon encouraging and empowering corruption. Cheney asked me how the White House staff was going to be structured, and I presented the spokes of the wheel model of equal presidential access by all presidential assistants.

Cheney said, "Are you telling me that Carter isn't going to have a chief of staff?" I remember saying that this was the plan, although there was an assumption that Hamilton Jordan was "best of" among equals, and he would command higher responsibility and power than the others. And Cheney said, "But no chief of staff." And I answered, "Right, no chief of staff."

After the New Year, early in January, I met again with Cheney in the White House. After our meeting, he asked me if I had another minute. He then went to his closet and took out a bicycle wheel with all the spokes gnarled and twisted together. He handed it to me and said, "Give this to President Carter and tell him that this is what the spokes of the wheel model looks like in practice." Then he laughed heartily.

I took the bicycle wheel back to my old office at the Democratic National Committee that Hamilton Jordan was using during the transition. I walked into my office, with the pictures of my kids still on my desk, and handed the bicycle with its gnarled and twisted spokes to him, saying "This is what Dick thinks of the spokes of the wheel structure." We both laughed. Then Hamilton said, "I'm afraid he's right, but that's what Jimmy wants."

I served in the White House as deputy assistant to the president, reporting to Hamilton Jordan for the first year and a half of the Carter administration. True to the spokes of the wheel model, all the assistants to the president had equal access to Carter, although it was very clear that Jordan was the most important "spoke." But it was often chaotic—things slipped through the cracks, and the president was micromanaging details that were not worth his time.

Shortly after I left the White House, the spokes of the wheel model was abandoned. As Cheney had predicted, the "spokes" had become "twisted and gnarled." Hamilton Jordan was made chief of staff, and the pyramid hierarchical model style reigned supreme for the rest of the Carter presidency.

Who Will Call This Meeting to Order?
Mark Siegel

The new senior staff of the Carter administration trickled into the West Wing on Inauguration Day, 1977.

I went up to my second floor West Wing office at about two p.m., after being sworn in and given my White House credentials. My boss, Hamilton Jordan was on the first floor, directly below me and next to the Oval Office. Someone walked into my office and said that we were going to have a senior staff meeting in the Roosevelt Room at four p.m. and that I was to be there.

At 3:45 p.m., I walked downstairs and into the Roosevelt Room, in total awe of the surroundings—the Nobel Prize sitting on the shelf and the open door across from the Oval Office. I cautiously sat down at the long conference table. I believe I was the first person there. And I waited.

Slowly the assistants to the president, the special assistants, and the deputy assistants started to fill up the room and sit at the table. It was four p.m. We waited.

And we waited.

And we waited.

At about 4:20 p.m., Counselor to the President Robert Lipchitz very shyly said to the group, "Well, I guess I'm the oldest person at the table, so I guess I should call this meeting to order."

The confusion was palpable and embarrassing—but quite understandable.

President Carter had made a conscious decision, based on his reading of the causes of the Watergate scandal, that there should be open access to the president by the senior staff and no hierarchical decision-making.

In other words, he wanted a West Wing without a chief of staff. So, when the senior staff gathered in the Roosevelt Room at four p.m. on January 20, 1977, there actually was no one to convene and run the meeting. No one was in charge.

I was Hamilton Jordan's deputy, and I was sitting next to him that day. I whispered in his ear: "I hope the Russians are not monitoring this meeting, because if they are this is a perfect time for a first strike."

Hamilton laughed. He thought I was kidding.

I wasn't.

Andy Warhol Lunches in the White House Mess
Mark Seigel

I first encountered Andy Warhol when I purchased his first venture into politics in 1972. For what was then an outrageously expensive price of $750, I bought what I thought was an extraordinarily creative and toxic lithograph of Richard Nixon: a frightening vision in insipid green that looked like the portrait of Dorian Gray with the words "Vote McGovern" scrawled across the bottom in Andy Warhol's handwriting. The lithograph was signed and numbered on the back. It is now valued at over $50,000.

I reached out to Warhol again in 1976 when I was executive director of the Democratic National Committee (DNC) to see if he would consider doing a portrait of presidential candidate Jimmy Carter to be used to generate contributions to the presidential campaign. He agreed. I asked him if he could modify his signature policy on the piece and sign and number it on the front and not on the back as he did in the Nixon/McGovern portrait. He agreed. Subsequently all of Andy's many political portraits were signed and numbered on the front.

After Carter was sworn in as president in 1977, I got a call in my new West Wing office from Andy. During that conversation I asked him if he would like to join me for lunch in the White House mess, saying it was the least we could do to thank him for his help in the campaign. He seemed quite excited and asked if he could possibly bring guests. I happily agreed.

The following week Andy and two women joined me in the White House. I don't remember the names of the women, but I do remember that they were very striking, in a strange Warholian way—white hair, very vivid makeup, kind of bizarre clothes. Andy looked a bit strange (he always did), but he came to the White House dressed appropriately in a suit and tie.

We sat and talked and lunched in the White House mess chatting about politics, art, and current events. I had an absolutely great time and was somewhat amused by the looks of embarrassment tinged with pity that I seemed to be getting from my White House colleagues. I still regret not taking him into the Oval Office to meet President Carter. I'm sure the president would have loved it.

The following day a note from Andy was delivered to my office thanking me for hosting him and his guests at lunch. It included what he called "three small gifts." The first, rolled in a tube, was his famous portrait of Mao Zedong in black and purple on white, on which he had scrawled "To Mark Siegel from Andy Warhol" across the bottom. There were also two copies of his autobiography. I opened the first one and Andy had autographed it to me and had drawn various curves and wiggles on many pages. He had amusingly drawn a Campbell Soup can with my name on it. I thought the second book was more of the same and put it aside.

White House staff were required to turn in gifts of value to the White House Counsel. I dutifully brought the Mao Zedong lithograph to Robert Lipchitz's office and handed it over. Lipchitz unrolled the lithograph, looked at it, and said (to my amazement), "He wrote your name on it. It's worthless." I said, "Okay" and got out of the office fast.

Afterward I would retell the story to Special Trade Representative Robert Strauss, my friend and political mentor. In a classic Strauss retort, he said, "Leave it to Jimmy Carter to find the one dumb Jewish lawyer in America." Lipchitz wasn't dumb but obviously didn't know much about art. The worthless Mao is now worth $80,000.

By chance, a couple of months later, I opened the second copy of the autobiography that Andy Warhol had given me. There were twirls and scribbles, but on the cover page quite clearly was a drawing of a Campbell Soup can with a small sketch of the White House in its center.

It is the only piece of its kind ever done by Andy Warhol.

Two Check Marks

Jerry Austin

When I went to graduate school in public administration at New York University, I wish I had known that what I learned the first day in the first class was all I needed to know. I would have saved myself a year and a half of school.

Because on the first day of the first class, the instructor said, "I'm going to tell you something now. If you learn nothing else from me during this whole year, you'll learn this priority. Every single major project that an elected official does will have two check marks: one check mark is if it makes sense managerially, and the other check mark is if it makes sense politically."

"Let me give you an example. You need to do this road, the road is really important for whatever reason, however, it goes right through the Council President's ward—so you don't do the road."

I later realized that when you get in trouble is it usually because you don't have the two check marks—you may have one or the other, but you don't have both of them.

What I tell my students now is that getting the two check marks is the number one priority of a political consultant.

Salt and Pepper Politics
Tom Ingram

Tennessee governor Lamar Alexander was really balanced. For instance, Lamar's goal as governor was to raise family incomes in the state. To accomplish that, he had to improve the education system so that people would be qualified for better jobs. Then he had to recruit the better jobs for the better educated people. But to get the better jobs he had to create a better transportation system in the state.

So, Alexander strategically used his transportation commissioner to develop a plan for an improved transportation system off the interstate highways to equip communities to attract better jobs. But he would also work into the plan a road here and road there, where he needed to reward friends or get a vote. So, he'd salt and pepper it.

Alexander started with his vision, but his vision wasn't worth a damn if he couldn't get it done. And he did!

Honey, Don't Worry About It
Ike McLeese

I was just twenty-two years old when I first started working for U.S. senator "Fritz" Hollings as a staffer on Capitol Hill. Fritz had a really big booming voice.

The lady who was his assistant sat at a desk just outside his personal office. His voice was so loud that I am sure she heard every word he uttered.

Although I had worked for him in his campaign, I was still a little intimidated by the senator. One day he was in an unusually fine mood, so I decided to share an idea with him.

He responded by saying in his big booming voice, "That is the dumbest idea I have ever heard in my life! You're on the payroll for ideas like that?"

Needless to say, my ego was more than a bit deflated by his reaction.

When I come out of the office door, his assistant is standing there waiting for me.

"Honey, don't you worry about it," she told me, "You are the third person that the senator has said that to today—and the first person was the president of the United States."

It's Got to Be the Shirt
James Crounse

Sometimes in politics, people you respect do funny things under pressure.

In 1994–95, I took a break from my career as a national direct mail consultant and served as chief of staff to Senator Max Baucus from Montana. Max had served Montana in the House, and then won an upset Senate race by running a great campaign that featured his walk across the state. Max ended up serving Montana in the Senate for thirty-six years, the longest of anyone in the state's history, and then went on to become President Obama's ambassador to China.

The Senate can be a very busy, intense, and hectic place. I remember one Wednesday in particular.

On Wednesdays, when Congress was in session, we hosted a very early morning breakfast for all Montanans who were in Washington and wanted to visit with their members of Congress and staff.

Ahead of us was an insanely busy day. The Senate was in session, which meant Max had several floor votes, in addition to meetings all day long. That night we had a major fundraising dinner at a downtown Washington, D.C. hotel. Vice President Gore was going to be in attendance, which was a big deal. Baucus and Gore were not exactly the best of friends when Gore was in the Senate. Despite that, Gore agreed to headline the important fundraiser for Max's reelection campaign. It definitely added to the stress of the day.

I had a meeting at two p.m. with a young person in politics who was seeking my advice. Nancy, our front desk person called me, and told me my two o'clock appointment was in the reception area.

I went up to the front desk to greet him and then walked him back to my office for our meeting. It was a long runway of offices that ended at the senator's office—a big corner office in the Hart Senate Office Building.

As I walked to my office with my guest, I saw the senator standing in the doorway of his office without his shirt and tie on—he was just wearing a T-shirt and his suit pants. He was quite agitated and yelling, "Help me, I need help!" I was not sure who he was yelling at or why.

Our scheduler Brooke was right in front of him; his executive assistant Sarah was in an office nearby. Yet the yelling persisted and now he was looking at me.

I ushered my guest into my office and told him I'd be with him shortly. I walked Max back into his office, shut the door, and asked him what was wrong.

He told me to look in his bathroom. In the sink was his white dress shirt, it was submerged in soapy water, with an ink stain on the pocket that had now widened out. It looked like a tie-dyed shirt. I had to laugh to myself.

Max was quite distraught at this point. I asked him what his shirt size was. He told me 16/33. I told him to just relax, I'd fix things.

I walked out of his office, went over to my assistant Jim Messina (the same Jim Messina who went on to be President Obama's deputy chief of staff, run his 2012 reelection campaign, and become my dear friend).

I gave him $75 and told him to get to take a cab to Union Station as fast as he could. There was a shirt shop at the station, I told him to get a white dress shirt, 16/33, and get back as fast as he could. He took off like a flash on this critical mission.

I went back into Max's office, and he was still quite upset. I told him everything was going to be okay and that I sent Messina to get him a new shirt.

He was grateful and said, "Thank God you knew just what to do."

I was thinking that my parents would have been proud, all the lessons they taught me, the college degree, the law degree, fifteen years of political experience that all culminated into that critical moment where I knew exactly what to do.

Of course, it was the same thing almost anyone would have done.

With a new shirt, the day brightened for Max, the dinner was a big success. Max went on to win convincingly in the upcoming election.

As they say, "It's got to be the shirt."

Four Tires for Ten Bucks
David Heller

One day, William Donald Schaefer—the second-term governor of Maryland, the only Democrat in the state to officially endorse George H. Bush against Bill Clinton—is invited to speak at the United Nations. God only knows why the governor of Maryland was asked to speak at the United Nations.

Schaefer is the cheapest human being known to man—the cheapest. He's not wealthy, never been wealthy, and never had money at all.

Flashback: When I was a kid, my dad ran a department store called Stewart Company in downtown Baltimore. Schaefer had just been elected mayor and wanted to revitalize the downtown. When all of the department stores were moving from the city to the suburbs, he asked my dad to put all the money into reopening the downtown department store. My father did, and they held the big grand opening.

I'm there standing beside my dad, and it's supposed to be one of his proudest moments. They cut the ribbon, open the store, and Schaefer gives a speech welcoming everybody. He says that it is the first step in revitalizing downtown Baltimore. He says that Mr. Heller has done great work to help lift the city, and when he is done speaking, he says, "I will go and make the ceremonial first purchase in the store." Now mind you, the podium and stage for dignitaries is in the front of the store.

Schaefer jumps off the stage and walks all the way to the back of the store, goes all the to the clearance section, picks up the cheapest thing he can find, brings it back to the front, and says, "I'm making the inaugural first purchase."

My father turns to me and goes, "If everyone is like him, we're going to go bankrupt."

Fast-forward: Schaefer is in New York City, and he is staying four or five blocks away from the United Nations building. His chief of staff says, "We've got to go. Let's get a cab so we'll be there on time." But Schaefer says, "It's a beautiful day, we don't need to spend money on a cab, let's walk."

The chief of staff says, "Governor, we don't want to be late."

"Oh, it's alright, it's just a short walk. It's a beautiful day, let's save the people some money."

So, Schaefer starts walking with his entourage toward the UN. He gets about halfway there, and he sees this guy selling tires—four for ten dollars. He's mesmerized, absolutely mesmerized. "Four tires, ten bucks! This is the greatest deal ever!" But he cannot choose what four tires to get for ten dollars. He ends up being late to address the United Nations because he can't figure out the cheapest deal.

Do It Now!
David Heller

When William Donald Schaefer ran for governor of Maryland, he had the best slogan I've ever seen: "Schaefer. Do it Now!" And that's who he was: he never waited. When he was mayor of Baltimore, he walked around with this enormous cell phone. It looked like two large bricks taped together. Every time he'd see a pothole, he'd call the head of the Department of Public Works at home. "Hey, corner of Madison and 14th, big pothole, fix it right now!" That's how he was: do it now, do it now, do it now. The voters loved him.

When he became governor, Schaefer didn't move to the governor's mansion in Annapolis but stayed in his old house in Auburn and commuted every day. It was a tough commute and some days he would arrive really angry.

One day he comes into work, and he has a cabinet meeting very first thing. He says, "Where is my transportation secretary?"

The transportation secretary, Jim Lighthizer at the time says, "I'm right here, Governor."

"Mr. Lighthizer, do you know how many abandoned cars I saw alongside the road today?" Schaeffer asks.

"No, Governor, I don't."

"Well, it is a travesty! There are so many abandoned cars beside the road! This is a driving hazard! This is ugly, and we should have beautiful highways, and people should be able to come and go! I want those abandoned cars off the side of the road, understand?"

"Yes, Governor I do."

"I don't think you do, Mr. Lighthizer."

"Yes, Governor."

"When I drive to work, if I see a single abandoned car along the side of the road, you're fired. Do you understand that?"

"Yes, Governor I do."

"Good! I'm serious!"

"Yes, Governor, I understand."

"Oh, and Lighthizer, I'm taking a different route to work tomorrow."

Later on, Schaefer goes to Congress to testify about the transportation committee about Maryland's transportation needs. It is chaired by Maryland congressman Steny Hoyer. Hoyer has the hearing all teed up for Schaefer to come in and tell the committee exactly what Maryland needs.

The governor comes in and testifies, "Well, we need money to expand the Baltimore-Washington airport. It's too small. And we need money to expand Martin Airbase for air cargo. And we need money to dredge the harbor; we need a deepwater port. We need railroad expansion to transport the shipments. Congressmen, you know, the metro light rail needs to be expanded. We need to build a green line, yellow line in Prince George's County. I want to build a subway in Baltimore—we have one in Washington, D.C., so we should have one in Baltimore. And then I want to build an interstate highway between Baltimore and Annapolis because there isn't a direct route to get there. We also need money for bike paths. Bike paths are very important since people want to exercise, be healthy, and keep our roads clear."

Hoyer looks at him and says, "Governor, you need money for planes, ships, trains, subways, automobiles, and bikes. Can you give this committee any sense of priority? What's most important to you?"

Schaefer says, "God damn it! They're all priorities, that's why I'm here!"

A Little Chin Music
James Crounse

The highlight of my professional career as a direct mail consultant was working on the 2008 Obama presidential campaign. The candidate was inspiring, the campaign was as well run as any campaign I've ever been part of, and the results were historic.

After the campaign, my dear friend Jim Messina, who was the deputy campaign manager, asked if I would help the transition with the confirmation of the president's cabinet nominees, including getting Kansas governor Kathleen Sebelius confirmed as the new secretary of the Department of Health and Human Services.

As part of the process, I accompanied the governor to meetings with some of the key senators on the finance committee.

The most memorable meeting was with Republican senator Jim Bunning from Kentucky. Bunning was a former Major League Baseball pitcher who was dominant in the 1960's and was voted into the Baseball Hall of Fame, a significant and rare honor for a baseball player. Bunning was known as a tough and consistent pitcher. He pitched a perfect game in 1964, had another no-hitter, held strikeout records, and ended up winning 224 games.

As a senator, he was very conservative and had a reputation for being irascible. But I was looking forward to the visit because I was a huge baseball fan. I remembered Bunning from my childhood and could even imitate his pitching style.

I remember being ushered into his office with Governor Sebelius. I was looking around for baseball memorabilia and was trying to pay close attention to the conversation at the same time.

Bunning was very odd in this meeting. He was not friendly. He tried to ask tough questions that were frankly hard to follow, and he interrupted the governor several times.

Governor Sebelius was a great governor. But more than that, she is a wonderful person who is smart, charming, experienced, and very effective. She grew up in Ohio. Her father, John Gilligan, was a successful and well-liked politician. He taught political science at Xavier College, served in the U.S. House, was elected governor of Ohio, and ran USAID during the Carter years. He was known as a principled liberal with an acerbic wit.

Thankfully, the meeting with Bunning was not a long one. As we wrapped up the meeting and started to walk out, Bunning reached out his major league pitcher's hand to Governor Sebelius. He shook her hand and said, "I went to college at Xavier and took a political science class from your father. He gave me a bad grade and I'll never forget it."

I suppose it was Bunning reverting to his attitude as a tough pitcher and throwing the governor a little "chin music" as a payback for the bad grade her father gave him some fifty years before.

Sebelius was confirmed and went on to serve as an excellent HHS secretary. She helped pass the Affordable Care Act—Obamacare—into law. It was a significant achievement that has helped millions get and keep health insurance.

Bunning, well, let's just say, I did not witness a "Hall of Fame" performance.

A Good Bet
David Heller

The first time I met Corrine Brown, an African American congresswoman from Florida, I flew down from Washington, D.C., early in the morning, arranged to meet her for lunch, and booked myself for the last flight that day back home.

We had lunch together, we spent the afternoon together, and we hit it off right away. She decided she wanted to hire me.

She said, "I want you to spend the night. I want to show you around my district. I want to talk to you about getting this campaign up and running."

I said, "No problem, happy to do it. I said I just need to go to a drug store to get some overnight stuff, you know—toothbrush, toothpaste, that sort of thing."

She said, "Okay."

She picked me up and took me to a shopping center outside the state representative district she represented at the time. We're walking into this drug store at about 9:00 p.m. I said to her, "You should have a sticker so that people know who you are when they meet you. Something like 'I'm Corrine Brown, and I'm running for Congress.'"

She said, "This is Jacksonville, everybody knows me!"

I said, "Corrine, respectfully, maybe in your district they know you, but we're not in your district, so they don't know you."

She said, "You want to bet?"

I said, "Yeah, sure."

There is a woman behind the register at the drug store.

I said, "I've got twenty bucks says she doesn't know who you are."

She said, "You're on."

I get my stuff, and we walk up to the counter.

I said to the woman behind the register, "Do you know who this is?"

She said, "Well yes, that's Corrine Brown."

Corrine holds out her hand, "Give me that money!"

I give her twenty bucks.

There are two cops in the parking lot.

I said, "Double or nothing those cops don't know who you are."

She said, "It's your money."

I said, "Okay."

I ask the first officer, "Can you tell me who this person is that's standing next to me?"

He looks at Corrine and says, "She looks familiar, but no, I don't know who she is."

I said, "Give me back twenty bucks."

She looks at the cop and says, "Say my name! Tell him my name!"

The cops said, "Well, that's Corinne Brown."

She holds out her hands and goes, "Give me another twenty dollars!"

She said, "We can play this all night long if you want."

I said, "No, no, no, I'm not betting you anymore tonight!"

But in the long run, it turned out to be a pretty good bet.

I Don't Need Anything, But They Do
David Heller

A few years after Congresswoman Corrine Brown arrived in Congress, President Clinton was asking for money for NASA—a big appropriation for Cape Canaveral in Florida. It was going to be a very close vote. Every member of the Florida delegation, every Democrat in the delegation, had voiced their support for this expenditure. Except Congresswoman Corrine Brown from Jacksonville. So, Clinton sent the head of NASA over to her office.

Corrine called me up and said, "I need you to come to my office, I got some white guy trying to come over here to talk to me. I want you in the meeting."

I said, "Okay."

I walked over to the meeting and sure enough, it's the head of NASA. He came into her office, and it was me, the head of NASA, her chief of staff, and the congresswoman—both of whom were African American. The head of NASA made the case for why the congresswoman should be supporting this appropriation and how it was going to benefit Florida and create a lot of jobs. He added that everyone else in the delegation was on board.

The congresswoman said, "But what is it going to do for my people? What kind of jobs is it going to create for my people?"

Then the head of NASA talked about the number of African Americans employed at NASA.

She said, "I don't want to talk about people who are just employed, I want to talk about people in science. I want to talk about people who are in the space program. I want to talk about astronauts and physicists who have advanced degrees. How many African Americans do you have in those jobs?"

The head of NASA said, "I don't know."

She said, "I think you don't know because you don't want me to know the answer. If you want my support, I want you to create an astronomy program at Florida A&M University. That way African Americans can learn physics and astronomy and go into the space program at the highest levels, not the lowest levels."

They go back and forth and ultimately agree on the new program.

After the meeting was over, I turned to her and said, "That was so impressive what you did. I just have one suggestion for you."

"What?" she said.

I said, "Florida A&M University is 250 miles away from your district. It would be even better if you could do it for a school that's in your district."

She said, "You don't understand. I'm not doing this for me. I'm doing this for the young African American children of Florida. I'm trying to create a better life for them. I didn't come here to serve me, I'm fine. I don't need anything, but they do. Don't you ever forget that."

The appropriation created the program and she voted for it.

Liking Your Adversary

Jerry Austin

In 2000, I was living in South Carolina, and I was called by a friend of mine who was running an organization called Kids Vote. The purpose was increasing kids' knowledge of elections by having kids go with their parents to the polling places—and also encouraging their parents to vote because their kids are involved.

John McCain allowed his presidential campaign in Charleston, South Carolina to schedule an event on the aircraft carrier Yorktown, and Kids Vote had arranged for Senator McCain to have a separate press conference with South Carolina Kids Vote Representatives.

I was asked to help coordinate that press conference. After the senator was finished with his formal announcement on the aircraft carrier—mind you the aircraft carrier is the biggest thing I've ever seen in my life—he came and had a press conference with the young people there. He seemed very engaged.

I thanked him for coming and he asked me where I was from. I told him that I was originally from New York but had been in Ohio for a long time. He said, "I like John Glenn. We disagree a lot, but I really like him. He and Annie are really good people."

It was refreshing to hear someone who was an adversary speak in such glowing terms of a colleague.

Here's Your Yarmulke, Mr. Prime Minister
Lincoln Mitchell

The 2012 election in Georgia—the country that was once part of the Soviet Union, not the American state—was one of the strangest and most intense in which I have ever been involved. I was informally advising, kibitzing might be the more accurate term, for the opposition bloc, known as the Georgia Dream (GD). The GD was trying to wrest power from the United National Movement (UNM), which had been in power since 2004. The UNM had grown increasingly authoritarian in the years leading up to the election, while the GD was a broad coalition of opposition forces.

In the years preceding that election, I had been a prominent academic critic of the UNM and was a frequent commentator on Georgian politics in Georgian, American, and European media. Despite the role I had played in helping the UNM come to power, by 2012, I was widely disliked by the party and its supporters. I had grown accustomed to the stream of ad hominem attacks from the Georgian government and their supporters. This included the frequent, and laughably false, accusation that I was secretly working for the Kremlin. On at least one occasion, those attacks took a nasty anti-Semitic turn.

The leader of the GD, and the coalition's candidate for prime minister, was an eccentric and reclusive man named Bidzina Ivanishvili. He was the richest man in

Georgia and had accumulated a fortune of about six billion dollars after the collapse of the Soviet Union. Bidzina had never sought elected office before, but he had a good political mind, and was able to think several strategic moves ahead of his opponents and partners. His money gave him the convening power to bring together many of the best and smartest Georgian politicians into a coalition.

Bidzina also had his quirks. He lived in an enormous modernist home overlooking Tbilisi, Georgia's capital, which was known by many as the "James Bond House." Bidzina also had a collection of exotic animals at his summer place on the Black Sea. I still have video of me feeding his pet zebras while waiting for a meeting there to start. The Georgian billionaire also seemed genuinely curious about many things. For example, after he learned that I was a big baseball fan, he frequently asked me questions about the game. He was also an avid art collector and yoga practitioner who had an almost preternatural calm, a striking contrast to Georgia's president Mikheil Saakashvili, known to everyone as Misha, who could charitably be described as high energy, but manic would probably be a better word.

Misha and Bidzina hated each other. Although it was a parliamentary election with Misha not even on the ballot, everybody understood this race was between these two very different, and in their own way, very impressive men. The election was very competitive and very nasty. Bidzina had enough money to compete with the state resources that Misha and the UNM could access. During the extremely competitive election, the attacks against me continued, but did not bother me all that much. After all, that is politics. Ultimately, a prison abuse scandal came to light in the final days before the election and drove many voters to the opposition, and the GD won handily.

After Bidzina won, he was faced with many tasks. One of those tasks was to persuade western, and particularly American, policy makers that he was tolerant, and liberal. With this goal in mind, I came up with the idea of having him visit the major synagogue in Tbilisi to show that he understood Georgia to be a diverse place.

I also knew this event would appeal to politicians in the U.S. Unlike many countries in the region, Georgia has little history of anti-Semitism and has always treated its Jewish citizens well.

Several Jewish Americans who had been working on the campaign also liked the idea, so we met with the head rabbi of the synagogue, who was flattered and excited by the idea of a visit by the new Prime Minister. I knew Bidzina had tremendous respect for Jews and our traditions, so I was confident he would go along with the suggestion. He did, but he told me he did not want to do anything that would either embarrass himself because of his unfamiliarity with Jewish religious practice or that would offend any of the worshippers when he went to the synagogue.

I assured him neither of those things would occur.

The plan was for Bidzina to arrive at the synagogue on Friday night before services were to begin and then for the rabbi to greet him and let him address the congregation. My two Jewish American friends and I would wait outside and bring him to the rabbi when he arrived.

So, on Friday night, we got to the synagogue before services. Like many good New York political operatives, I usually have a yarmulke in my suit pocket, but I went inside anyway to get a few extras for Bidzina and his entourage. It was raining very hard that evening, but Bidzina arrived on time, trailed by television crews from most of Georgia's stations and surrounded by his security team of burly Georgians and Americans.

Bidzina got out of his car and walked directly to me. The cameras were now on both of us. I smiled, shook Bidzina's hand, and then reached into my pocket, handed him one of the yarmulkes, and said, "Here's your yarmulke, Mr. Prime Minister," explaining that he needed to wear it before he went inside the synagogue. He immediately put the yarmulke on his head.

However, when I passed yarmulkes out to his security team, there was a bit of grumbling. But one look from the new Prime Minister put an end to that.

Character Counts

William Sweeney

We all get involved with campaigns and candidates for a spectrum of reasons. In 2004, Susan Sweeney volunteered for Wes Clark's campaign for the Democratic presidential nomination. In addition to respect for Wes's positions on issues and history of leadership, he had also had a neighborhood connection from Churchill Road Elementary School in McLean, Virginia.

On August 19, 1995, a NATO military convoy proceeded along a narrow, rain-soaked road by Mount Igman to Sarajevo. This road was the only one not controlled by the Bosnian Serbs and the route had been repeatedly subject to both artillery and machine-gun fire. The first armored personnel carrier included Richard Holbrooke and NATO Commander Wes Clark. The second armored personnel carrier carried three American diplomats—Robert Frasure, Joseph Kruzel, and S. Nelson Drew, accompanied by French soldiers.

Officially, the road collapsed due to the weight of the armored personnel carrier. The second vehicle dropped five hundred meters down the mountain and then exploded due to ammunition igniting in the vehicle. Two American diplomats (Frasure and Drew) died in the vehicle along with some French soldiers, while Kruzel and others were thrown free of the vehicle, but all were fatally wounded in the accident.

Wes Clark, the NATO Commander, wrapped a rope around himself and scaled the mountain side, ignoring the protests of Holbrooke and others. Reportedly, there were concerns about snipers as well as the safety of the NATO Commander.

Kruzel had died by the time Clark reached him. Clark collected Kruzel's personal effects, including his gold wedding ring.

Holbrooke and Clark accompanied the bodies back to Washington, D.C.

Portrait of a Political Insider

Ira Forman

James B. King died Sunday, June 8, 2019, while working at his home in Rockport, Massachusetts. He was 84. We lost one of the great practitioners of American politics. To paraphrase the tagline from the 1960s TV drama *Naked City*, there are eight million hilarious and inspiring stories in American politics. James B. King stars in nearly all of them.

As a teenager Jim King volunteered for John F. Kennedy's 1952 Senate race. His career included working for all three Kennedy brothers and for Senator John Kerry, too. He become the premier advance man in American politics, serving as the guru for generations of Democratic political operatives.

There are many great résumés in Washington, D.C. But very few of those résumés are linked to an individual who was a sage of American politics, who embodied the power of laughter, who personified commitment to public service and treated everyone he met with the respect and dignity all human beings deserve. Jim led the Office of White House Personnel, chaired the National Transportation Safety Board, served as Director of the Office of Personnel Management (OPM), and also served as a vice president at Harvard and Northeastern universities.

Jim forgot more about American politics than any of the rest of us—his students in politics—would ever learn. He could teach you every trick in the book of political advance. He could walk into a bar in any American town, and by the time he finished one beer, he could tell you what issues moved the locals. If his candidate had an unconscious habit of grabbing his privates (true story), Jim could figure out how to situate the spouse on the campaign trail so she could stand next to her candidate husband and hold the offending hand when he was on a podium.

Oh, the stories—stories told by Jim and stories told about Jim.

There was the time he worked on the 1967 campaign to elect Richard Hatcher as the first African American mayor of a large American city. Hatcher was running in Gary, Indiana, to unseat a corrupt, political machine. The Hatcher campaign had no poll watchers to protect against ballot box stuffing. The only asset Jim had to work with was large numbers of volunteer college students. Jim scoured the local Goodwill and Salvation Army stores to find black suits, sunglasses, and black fedoras to dress his student to look like FBI agents stationed outside polling places. Needless to say, there were no stuffed ballot boxes that Election Day in Gary that election. Hatcher beat the machine.

For Jim, politics was not about self-aggrandizement. The first time I attended a Jim King staff meeting at OPM, he nixed the idea of getting a puff piece on his career published in *The Washington Post*. He told us that the way to get things done in Washington, D.C., was not to seek the spotlight for yourself, but to look for ways to give credit to others.

I will never forget a House Appropriations Subcommittee Hearing in the spring of 1995. The new GOP majority in the House and the Clinton Administration agencies were often at loggerheads, and the OPM staff was concerned that our budget was about to be slashed.

Jim gave a typical Jim King opening statement where he outlined the importance of improving and protecting the civil service while using self-deprecating humor to make his points. The Republican subcommittee chair, Representative Lightfoot of Iowa, then opened his remarks by praising Jim as one of the rare and refreshing breed of Washington officials who take their mission seriously, but do not take themselves so seriously. Our budget requests were not slashed that day.

But what made Jim particularly special was his humanity. Jim never forgot where he came from—a working-class Irish Catholic Democrat from Ludlow, Massachusetts. As proud as he was of his roots, he believed in giving the deepest respect and kindness to everyone he met, no matter their backgrounds.

While working for Jim at OPM in 1994, my father unexpectedly died. I went to see Director King to seek his permission that I be allowed to take my lunch hours off (if it did not conflict with a congressional hearing) so I could attend a Jewish service and say the Kaddish prayer—the Hebrew prayer one says for a deceased loved one.

Jim, to my initial surprise, answered me by saying, "No, Ira you do not have my permission." He then paused a moment and said, "You do not have my permission, but you do have my order: you are to go every day to services and honor your father. And I do not want to ever see you on the job during that time of the day no matter what else is going on."

To quote William Shakespeare, we "shall not look upon his like again." But we can all take lessons from his life to defend and strengthen the American democracy he loved.

The Battleship Campaign
Tony Fazio

This story is about my working with Dianne Feinstein, then the mayor of San Francisco, and her fight to make her city the permanent home port for battleship U.S.S. *Missouri*—on whose deck the Japanese surrendered to end the World War II.

Mayor Feinstein called me when she needed help with her "Home Port of the Missouri Campaign." I was not on the mayor's Christmas Card list because I had once worked for an opponent Feinstein had run against and won. But she had come to respect the work that my company did, and I agreed to do some lobbying, signs, and literature for the battleship campaign.

Mayor Feinstein was a fierce competitor, and she was taking on a large segment of the progressive community in San Francisco and the Bay Area. Although the campaign was not successful, I believe that it set her up for a successful run for a U.S. senator seat, where she served alongside Senator Barbara Boxer. I worked on both those campaigns.

After Mayor Feinstein lost the battleship campaign, she invited me to have lunch with her and the Deputy Mayor Hadley Roff. I showed up at the Washington Square Bar and Grill, then the political hotspot in town. I had been there many times with friends—but never with the mayor of San Francisco.

I was extremely nervous. She was very attentive, complimenting me on my assistance to her on the campaign. She asked me to order whatever I would like—it was her treat. I did not feel much like eating, but to be polite, I ordered a house special steak. They brought our lunch, and we continued chatting.

Then she said in a very motherly fashion, "You are not eating," and proceeded to cut my steak into bite-sized portions so it would be easier for me to eat.

Well, you can imagine my surprise. I looked around the room to see if anyone was watching besides me and the deputy mayor, whom it did not seem to faze at all. I just took it in stride, thanked her, and ate my lunch.

Mayor Feinstein was a very tough woman but a very classy lady. She could be very warm and charming when she wanted to be.

One Tough Woman
Gary Brody

Muriel Faye "Mickie" Siebert came to Wall Street from Ohio in 1954, a few credits shy of a degree from Case Western Reserve University. In a few short years, she became an expert in the airline industry stocks, one of the least preferred industry sectors. She rose to become the first woman to own a seat on the NYSE and the owner of one of the very first discount brokerage firms. She was dubbed the "First Woman of Finance."

When Hugh Carey, a Democrat, became governor of New York, he was looking for a smart, tough Republican woman to regulate New York State chartered banks. Mickie became the superintendent of Banking. I was her deputy.

She was an authentic character. She fought her way into River House, which did not want another Jewish resident at the time. They already had Henry Kissinger. But other residents like Jimmy Robinson III, chairman of American Express; Walter Wriston, the chairman of Citibank; and Leon Hess, the owner of the New York Jets and Hess Oil all went to bat for her.

She was a tough leader, committed to the Community Investment Act and anti-redlining enforcement. She was also involved as the regulator of branches of foreign company banks from China and Iran.

This was a major transitional moment in banking. The Glass-Steagall Act, which prohibited nationally chartered banks from investing depositor's money in stocks and bonds, was repealed. Mickie didn't think it was a good idea for banks to be involved in "stocks and socks," and did not want to give comparable powers to state-chartered institutions. Also, at this time the savings bank industry was imperiled. Their portfolios were comprised of home mortgages granted over thirty years at the then current rates.

Mickie was a tiger fighting with the Federal Deposit Insurance commission chairman, Bill Isaacs, chairman of the Federal Reserve, Paul Volcker, and New York's U.S. senators Chuck Schumer and Patrick Moynihan.

It was all to no avail.

So, she began the painful process of liquidating an industry. Week after week on Friday at 3 p.m. our examiners would appear at each branch, take possession, and post signs that the bank would open on Monday under new ownership. We meanwhile would meet with the bank's board and transfer the bank's ownership.

The bank boards were very gracious to Mickie, recognizing how valiantly she had fought for another solution for their salvation. When it was over, Mickie and I would head downtown to Sammy's Deli, where they would be waiting for us, even though it would likely be one or two a.m. They would have fishbowls full of vodka where we would drown our unhappiness. Then she would have the chauffeur take her back to River House and have him drive me home to Long Island.

Mickie's ultimate follow-up was challenging Senator Moynihan for his reelection in 1982. She finished second in the Republican primary to State Assemblywoman Florence Sullivan, who went on to lose to Moynihan in the general election.

We Didn't Save Milly
Mark Siegel

Early in my career at the Democratic National Commitee (DNC), Judy and I were invited to a dinner party at the home of journalist Morton Kondracke, then with the *Chicago Tribune,* and his wife, Milly Kondracke, a social psychologist. As a reporter Mort had followed my career at Northwestern, Loyola, and in Democratic politics. The dinner party was at the Kondracke home in Chevy Chase, Maryland.

Milly Kondracke was an eclectic and electric personality, the child of a Jewish mother and a Mexican communist father. She was fiercely independent and never hesitated in sharing her opinion, even if that meant confronting a government or political official, sometimes right in her own home.

I remember that first dinner at the Kondracke home very clearly for two reasons. It was the first time that I had ever eaten chicken mole, fascinated by what seems the very strange concept of adding chocolate to meat (Milly, on top of all her other achievements, was an outstanding Mexican cook). Second, there were two other guests at that dinner who were becoming increasingly well known for their work for *The Washington Post* covering the Watergate break-in and cover-up. Their names, now with a pivotal place in American history, were Carl Bernstein and Bob Woodward.

At some point in the evening Mort must have mentioned to them that I had worked for Hubert Humphrey during his presidential campaign and was an associate of Archer Daniels Midland CEO Dwayne Andreas. Andreas was the source of the $25,000 in cash that was given to the Committee to Reelect Richard Nixon and was used to pay for the Watergate break-in. They latched on to me that night and would not let go, peppering me with question after question about Andreas, Humphrey, and campaign finances. I had dealt with reporters before but never any as aggressive as the Woodward and Bernstein team. I told them what I knew and confirmed some things they suspected. It was an experience. They were suffocating. They were like persistent parasites leeching on to skin. I was glad to cooperate just to get them off my back.

After that first dinner party Mort and Milly and Judy and I became increasingly close friends. I guess it was clear that the Siegels and Kondrackes could accurately be described as "best friends." We moved into their neighborhood just a couple of blocks from the Kondracke home. Our children grew up together. We shared every Thanksgiving and Passover together. Our son Robert and the Kondracke daughter Andrea even ran as a ticket for president and vice president of Leland Junior High School. (I supplied the political campaign buttons). We frequently ate together and played together. We cooked together and went to the movies together.

At one memorable little diner party Mort and Milly invited me and Judy and Lynn and Dick Cheney. The dinner party sharply turned away from civility to contention when Lynn Cheney began spouting conservative (hard right-wing) dictates on public education. Milly and I were especially hard on her. When Judy raised the question of the lack of special education programs throughout the South, in particular the state of Florida, Mrs. Cheney curtly said, "If people aren't happy with their state's education systems, then they should just move." Milly Kondracke pounced on her, "How about government providing necessary services?"

The Kondrackes had personal reasons to be concerned about special education programs. Their daughter Andrea had difficulty in school. Some elementary and junior high school teachers and administrators suggested she was mildly retarded. Milly Kondracke knew better and fought them with hell fire. She made it exceedingly clear to Montgomery County Maryland school administrators that her daughter was very bright and obviously had a learning disability that had to be dealt with and overcome. Finally, after Milly's incessant demands, Andrea Kondracke was tested and found to be dyslexic. After the diagnosis she blossomed in her studies, going on to be an honors graduate of Boston College and later receiving her MD from Johns Hopkins Medical School, one of the greatest medical schools in the world. She is now Director of Child Psychiatry at Bellevue Medical Center in New York and a nationally recognized leader in her field. We owe all of this to Milly, a woman who would not stop fighting, a woman who would never accept limits, a woman who was fearless and feisty.

In 1990, Milly started to have trouble with writing and with balance. Our daughter Rebecca helped her address envelopes and write checks. The condition worsened and was eventually diagnosed as Parkinson's disease. Milly's conditioned dramatically deteriorated over the years. Her form of the disease was extremely rare and was diagnosed as "Parkinson's Plus." Month by month she lost more control of her body. She could not walk. She was unable to speak. She and Mort went all over the United States for the most state-of-the-art treatments, including some that were experimental and controversial. At Duke University, she underwent a novel brain procedure that had had some promising results with other Parkinson's patients, but unfortunately Milly's condition continued to deteriorate.

One of the most promising potential treatments that could stop and reverse Parkinson deterioration was embryonic stem cell research. This type of innovative research was being blocked by legislation and executive action of Republican presidents, governors, congressmen, and senators.

Judy and I and Mort and Milly moved from living a few blocks away from each other in Chevy Chase to living a few blocks away from each other in the Kalorama section of Washington, D.C. We saw each other often. We had dinner together every few weeks, although Milly could no longer eat regular food and could not communicate verbally. Somehow, she and I managed to work out our own form of communication, maybe because we knew each other so well, and also shared liberal Democratic politics and could read each other's minds. I could easily predict what she was thinking, and she would indicate with her eyes whether she agreed or disagreed. It was remarkable. One of the subjects we talked about was advances in Parkinson research abroad and the possibility that stem cells could be used to arrest the disease as they had successfully been used in other diseases.

During that time Mort wrote a bestselling book entitled "Saving Milly." The book was made into a television movie. It drew attention to Milly's struggle and courage. And just as important, it drew attention to Parkinson's disease.

Judy and I also noticed that as Milly's diseased progressed, many if not most or our mutual friends seemed to disappear rather than confront the reality of Milly's deteriorating life. I recall one masquerade party in Washington, D.C., where Milly came dressed as Franklin D. Roosevelt, in her wheelchair, with a long cigarette holder dangling from her mouth. Even in her tragic situation she maintained a remarkable courage and sense of humor. But at that large party Milly's wheelchair was in a room, and all our friends stayed away. Literally no one came to sit with us. No one came to try to talk to Milly. The party lasted for three hours. I never left her side. Maybe that moment rekindled the loneliness I had felt as a child, growing up in household of silence. But I would not let Milly be ignored. I talked. Her eyes answered. We didn't need the others who didn't have the courage or decency to trouble themselves with trying to be human.

Over the ensuing months Milly drifted away. She became nonresponsive. Those of us who loved her sat with her and talked to her and read to her, hoping that she was hearing us and hoping that we were giving her some comfort.

Milly Kondracke died on July 22, 2004, immediately prior to the Republican National Convention in New York City. Her funeral and memorial service was postponed until after the convention was over because so many of Milly and Morton's friends and associates had to be in New York. Parkinson's had become my passion during Milly's struggle, and I would do anything to raise the profile of the disease, its prevention, and hopefully its treatment. Toward that end I had gotten my friend Ron Reagan (yes, the president's son) to deliver a powerful prime-time speech at the Democratic National Convention on embryonic stem cell research. Because of who he was, the speech drew enormous attention. Ron's mother, former First Lady Nancy Reagan, publicly and strongly endorsed Ron's message.

The memorial service for Milly Kondracke was held in Georgetown in Washington, D.C. at St. Columbus' Episcopal Church. Mort asked me to deliver one of the eulogies. The church was full of Washington's political, governmental, and media establishment. I knew who was in the room. In the pews of that church were our nation's "power elite," those who make policy, those who write laws, those who supervise and fund medical research. I knew Milly. I knew that she would want me to seize the day.

I began my eulogy with what I think were stunning, unexpected words, the semantic counter to Morton's book title. To a hushed church I said, in a strong, maybe even angry voice: "WE DIDN'T SAVE MILLY." I proceeded to catalogue the fourteen years of Milly's suffering, her courage, and her dignity. I referenced the abandonment of so many who could not cope with Milly's tragedy and chose to avoid it and avoid her. And then I looked out into the church, and I saw Senator Elizabeth Dole of North Carolina. I saw Andy Card, chief of staff to the president of the United States. I saw the people who had the power to allow critical research on Parkinson's, but because of fear from the Republican right-to-life base blocked the most promising tool available to science—embryonic stem cell research.

Looking out at them I turned a loving eulogy into a rousing call for political action. My cadence increased, and my voice grew stronger. I repeated the line "We didn't save Milly," but then I added, "but in her name we can save thousands, maybe millions of those who suffer with Parkinson's disease. In her name we can save millions of children who are doomed by juvenile diabetes, millions more cursed by the living hell of Alzheimer's. We didn't save Milly, but we can save them."

The church erupted in applause, and then people rose, and then they cheered. It was a eulogy that became a campaign speech. I was as shocked as the congregants.

Later that day Mort Kondracke received a call from the White House. The White House chief of staff Andy Card wanted to meet with Mort to see if they could agree on some steps, some progress on stem cell research. I think those discussions led to an adjustment in U.S. policy permitting stem cell research using embryos not from abortions but rather from an IVP pool of embryos that would otherwise have been discarded.

It was a reasonable compromise. At least it was a start. Was the response by the White House and Republican senators a function of guilt, social responsibility, or politics? Whatever characteristic of human nature that triggered action is irrelevant. It is another example of the intervention of unexpected chance impacting policy and history, of seizing the moment to take a stand and hopefully make a difference.

I'm not really that proud of many things that I have done in my life. I have passed many tests but failed many others. I always think I could have and should have done more. But one of the things I am most proud of was turning a eulogy into a battle cry for research that could save lives.

I didn't save Milly. But when given a fortuitous opportunity, I did something.

About the Contributors

Gerald "Jerry" Austin is one of the nation's most experienced and successful political strategists. Austin has consulted on races throughout the United States at every level from precinct committee person to president of the United States. Raised in the Bronx, Austin learned his politics in Cleveland in the late 1960s. After helping elect Richard Celeste as governor of Ohio twice, he became the campaign manager for Reverend Jesse Jackson's 1988 presidential campaign. He was the senior political director for Paul Tsongas's 1992 campaign for president and helped elect Paul Wellstone to the United States Senate. In 1992, he was the consultant and media adviser for Carol Mosely Braun's historic campaign for the U.S. Senate. His work also includes witnessing the Marcos/Aquino election in the Philippines; the Pinochet plebiscite in Chile; and many trips to Northern Ireland to consult for the SDLP party. Austin earned a BA in American History from the City College of New York; a master's in Public Administration from New York University; and a master's in Education from The University of Akron. He served as an adjunct professor and director of the International Campaign Fellows program at The Bliss Institute of Applied Politics at The University of Akron.

Corey Bush has worked as a political consultant with experience in local, state, and national elections. He served as administrative assistant to California state senate majority leader George R. Moscone, and then as press secretary and chief speechwriter when Moscone was mayor of San Francisco. He was also a consultant to Major League Baseball commissioner Bud Selig as well as executive vice president of the San Francisco Giants

Gary Brody is a longtime lobbyist for New York state bankers. He served as executive assistant to the Superintendent of Banking and later as Deputy Superintendent of Banking. He stayed in the banking field representing the Savings Banks Association and the Community Bankers Association of New York State.

Terry Casey is a Republican political consultant and pundit based in Ohio. He has worked over five decades with state legislators, judges, mayors, state officeholders, and community groups, doing research and media on various public policy issues.

Bill Cohen spent forty years as a political reporter for the Ohio Statehouse News Bureau, affiliated with public radio. He retired in 2013.

James Crounse is recognized as one of the top Democratic mail consultants in the country. He has produced winning and creative political direct mail and provided strategic counsel to Democratic candidates for over thirty years. His clients included U.S. senators such as Evan Bayh, Chris Dodd, and Kristen Sinema, as well as President Barack Obama.

Mike Curtin spent more than thirty years working for the *Columbus Dispatch*, beginning as a reporter in 1973, becoming a political reporter in 1982, then serving as public affairs and managing editor before retiring as associate publisher emeritus in 2007. He then served two terms in the Ohio State House of Representatives.

Tom Diemer covered Ohio politics for many decades as a reporter with the Associated Press and the *Cleveland Plain Dealer*, where he served in the Columbus and Washington, D.C., bureaus. He teaches in the Washington Program of Northwestern University's Medill School of Journalism.

Tony Fazio is the founder of the direct mail firm Winning Directions. He has over forty years of experience working on hundreds of campaigns in the political communications industry, including candidates, labor organizations, and issue campaigns across America.

Bill Fletcher is CEO and partner of Fletcher Ridge & Co. He is a writer, photographer, musician, and film/video director. He has worked on hundreds of political and corporate campaigns across the U.S. and internationally. Bill excels in strategic communications and the production of high-quality multimedia projects.

Ira Forman started his career in 1977 working as a legislative liaison for AIPAC and stayed until 1981. After completing his MBA, he went to work for the National PAC, was a fellow with the Center for National Policy, executive director of the National Jewish Democratic Council, and Jewish outreach director for President Obama's 2012 Reelection Campaign.

Les Francis served as the first chief of staff for the late Congressman Norman Mineta before moving to Jimmy Carter's White House as deputy assistant to the president and eventually deputy White House chief of staff. He remained active in national politics and public affairs from offices in Washington, D.C., for four decades before returning to his native California in 2016.

Joe Hallett covered Ohio politics for the *Toledo Blade, Cleveland Plain Dealer,* and *Columbus Dispatch* for forty-two years. He retired in 2014 as senior editor for the *Columbus Dispatch.*

David Heller is one of the top political media consultants and campaign strategists in the Democratic Party. As president of Main Street Communications, an award-winning political media firm, Dave has compiled the best win-loss record in the Democratic Party, helping clients win election to Congress.

Bill Hershey spent forty years covering Ohio politics for the *Dayton Daily News* and the *Akron Beacon Journal*, where he served as Columbus Bureau chief and Washington, D.C., correspondent. He retired in 2012.

Tom Ingram founded the Ingram Group after leaving his post as deputy to the governor and chief of staff to then governor Lamar Alexander. Tom realized if he could do anything, he'd hang a shingle and put up a sign that said, "Crisis manager, problem solver."

Celinda Lake is a leading pollster and political strategist, serving as tactician and senior adviser. Celinda is president of Lake Research Partners, which is known for cutting-edge research on issues including the economy, health care, the environment, and education.

Lee Leonard covered Ohio politics for *United Press International and the Columbus Dispatch*, with a focus on the Ohio State legislature, and published pieces in *Columbus Monthly, Ohio Magazine*, and *State Legislatures Magazine.* He retired in 2005.

Bob Leonard is the news director of KNIA/KRLS radio in Pella, Knoxville, and Indianola and has covered politics since 2007. He interviewed every 2020 presidential candidate, appeared on national TV shows, and wrote for the *New York Times* about politics in rural Iowa.

Joanne Limbach is a specialist in state and local state policy. Limbach served as tax commissioner for the State of Ohio-Ohio Department of Taxation and member of the cabinet of Governor Richard F. Celeste. She is past president of the Federation of Tax Administrators and a former director of government affairs for The Success Group, Inc.

Ike McLeese was the president and CEO of the Greater Columbia Chamber of Commerce in South Carolina, after long experience in South Carolina campaign politics. He passed away in 2013.

Tim Miller covered Ohio politics for *United Press International* (serving as Ohio State Editor) and the *Dayton Daily News* (serving as Statehouse Bureau Chief). He is vice president of the Cochran Group, a public relations and communications firm in Columbus, Ohio.

Lincoln Mitchell is a political analyst, pundit, and writer based in New York City and San Francisco. He works on democracy and governance related issues in the U.S. and around the world. He is an accomplished scholar and writer whose current research includes democratic rollback in the U.S., the political history of San Francisco, U.S.-Georgia relations, political development in the former Soviet Union, the role of democracy promotion in American foreign policy, and baseball.

Dan Mowbray is a retired independent broadcast media professional who previously wrote for the *Columbus Dispatch*.

Bob Mulholland is a California based political activist. He was a senior adviser to the California Democratic Party from 1991 to 2010. From 1992, he was a political consultant to Tony Blair and the Labour Party (UK).

Bob Ney was a member of the Ohio State House of Representatives (1981–1982), Ohio state senate (1984–1995), and the U.S. House of Representatives (1995–2006). He is a political analyst for Talk Media News.

Phil Noble is recognized globally as one of the leading experts on uses of the Internet in the civic sector—in politics, media, government, and public affairs. In 1996, Noble founded Politics Online, the premier international company providing news, tools, and strategies for the civic sector globally. Noble was a Democratic candidate for lieutenant governor of South Carolina in 1994 and was a Democratic candidate for governor of South Carolina in 2018.

John Polidori has worked in a wide variety of political and legislative campaigns at the national, state, and local levels for more than four decades. This work has taken him to twenty-eight different states. His consulting work has encompassed elections, referenda, and legislative (public policy) campaigns. His union work comprised varied experiences as an organizer, contract/grievance negotiator, lobbyist, media relations consultant, political/elections specialist, and public policy analyst/adviser.

Katherine Rogers was a Democratic Party member of the New Hampshire House of Representatives, having served from 2012 to 2020 and 1992 to 1998, and previously in various local offices. She had extensive experience in campaigns across the country. She passed away in 2022.

Steve Rosenthal is an American labor and political strategist. He served for seven years as the political director of the AFL-CIO, stepping down in August 2002. At the time, the *New York Times* reported that many union leaders credited Rosenthal with "transforming organized labor's feeble, forgettable campaign operation into one that many political analysts say is the most effective in the nation."

Mary Anne Sharkey covered Ohio politics for *The Journal Herald* and *Cleveland Plain Dealer,* where she served as Columbus bureau chief and Politics and Opinion editor. She was the first woman elected president of the Ohio Legislative Correspondents Association. She is a fellow at Harvard University's Institute of Politics.

Hank Sheinkopf is president of Sheinkopf Communications, a full-service strategic communications company serving corporate, political, and public affairs clients. He has worked on an estimated seven hundred political campaigns on four continents, in fourteen foreign nations and forty-four American states over the last thirty-five years.

Mark Siegel is a Democratic Party activist and White House official. He was executive director of the Democratic National Committee under the chairmanship of Robert S. Strauss, the first Jewish chairman of a major American political party (1973–77). Siegel became deputy assistant to President Jimmy Carter in January 1977. Siegel later served as president of Mark A. Siegel and Associates, Inc., and International Public Strategies, Inc., lobbying firms dealing with domestic and international representation.

Rick Silver formed Chernoff/Silver & Associates in 1976 after serving as an aide for two lieutenant governors. Since then, his ideas have gotten bigger and better in a wide variety of fields—from education, healthcare, and economic development to energy, the environment, and insurance. Rick's reputation precedes him as an expert in research methodology and analysis, opinion polling, issues management, and public relations.

William Sweeney was the president and chief executive officer of the International Foundation for Electoral Systems (IFES) from 2009–2018. He served as deputy chairman of the National Democratic Committee, executive director of the Democratic Congressional Campaign Committee, and part of the management team for seven U.S. presidential inaugurations.

Donald R. Sweitzer is one of The Campaign Group's founders and is a veteran of two presidential campaigns. Don has successfully elected more than thirty members of Congress and statewide elected officials. He brings a special expertise in media targeting and is a regular guest lecturer across the country on political strategy and media planning. He is the former political director of the Democratic National Committee and the former chairman of IGT Global.

Sandy Theis covered Ohio politics for more than three decades with the Horvitz papers, the *Cincinnati Enquirer* (including as Columbus bureau chief) and the *Cleveland Plain Dealer* (including was Statehouse bureau chief). She is the owner of Theis Research & Consulting LLC in Dublin, Ohio.

Paul Tipps was an Ohio Democratic Party leader, serving as the chair of the Montgomery County Democratic Party (1970–1976); chair of the Ohio Democratic Party (1976–1983), and a lobbyist with State Street Consultants, Columbus. He passed away in 2015.

Joe Trippi is an American political strategist who has worked on several gubernatorial, U.S. States Senate and House races, including Jerry Brown for governor of California and Doug Jones for U.S. Senate in Alabama. He has worked for several Democratic presidential campaigns, most notably as manager of the Howard Dean 2004 presidential campaign.

Gerry Tyson is president of the Tyson Organization in the Dallas/Fort Worth area. After spending more than a decade with another firm, Gerry Tyson founded The Tyson Organization in 1983 and has since served Democratic and progressive clients in fifty states, planning and executing telephone-based programs for campaigns at the local, state and federal levels.

David Yepsen covered politics for the *Des Moines Register* for thirty-four years and became its political columnist in 2000. He became director of the Paul Simon Public Policy Institute at Southern Illinois University in 2009 before retiring in 2016.

Mark Weaver is the founder of Communications Counsel, a crisis communications expert with three decades of experience advising clients in twenty-five states and at the highest levels of national government and major corporations. He served as the deputy attorney general of Ohio, and on the attorney general's executive staff as a senior policy adviser and chief spokesman.

Jim Underwood covered Ohio politics for the Horvitz papers and the *Cleveland Plain Dealer* for more than two decades. In 1993, he founded Underwood & Associates, a research analysis firm, and began teaching journalism at Ohio Wesleyan University.

Abe Zaidan was a professional journalist and freelance writer in Ohio for more than forty years, serving as a political reporter and columnist for the *Akron Beacon Journal*, and Ohio correspondent for *The Washington Post*. He passed away in 2021.

Neal (Nick) Zimmers served in the Ohio state senate from 1975 to 1994. He is president of Zimmers and Associates, a government relations and political consulting firm.

John Zogby is Senior Partner, John Zogby Strategies. Over four decades, he was one of the most accurate pollsters in the world, conducting business in eighty countries, and leading the way in finding the meaning, story, direction, and usefulness of the data collected.

Printed in the United States
by Baker & Taylor Publisher Services